THE MYTH
AND REALITY
OF JUDAISM

82 MISCONCEPTIONS SET STRAIGHT

THE MYTH AND REALITY OF JUDAISM

82 MISCONCEPTIONS SET STRAIGHT

RABBI SIMON GLUSTROM

BEHRMAN HOUSE PUBLISHERS

Published by Behrman House, Inc.
235 Watchung Ave.
West Orange, NJ 07052

Typesetting and Design by RCC.

Library of Congress Cataloging-in-Publication Data

Glustrom, Simon
        The myth and reality of Judaism : 82 misconceptions set
straight / by Simon Glustrom
        p. cm.
        ISBN 0-87441-479-2
        1. Judaism--Miscellanea.   I. Title.
BM51.G56   1988
296--dc19   88-34610
                                                                        CIP

Helen and I dedicate this book
to our grandchildren

Jonathan Aaron
Daniel Alexander
Jonah Abraham
Zoe Rebecca

With deep love and high hopes

PREFACE, *page xi*

ACKNOWLEDGMENTS, *page xix*

BASIC BELIEFS *What Jews Really Believe, page 1*

1 The Jews constitute a race **2** Judaism is a religion **3** Belief in miracles is essential to the Jewish faith **4** Unlike Christians, Jews were never required to accept dogmas **5** The main function of the Hebrew prophets was to predict the future **6** Saints have no place in Jewish thought **7** Belief in the Chosen People implies superiority over other peoples **8** Belief in a Satan was always alien to Judaism **9** Judaism completely rejects the monastic or ascetic life **10** Judaism discourages controversy and debate **11** The theory of Evolution is incompatible with Jewish thought **12** The main goal of religious belief is to provide peace of mind

GOD *Questioning Familiar Views, page 37*

13 Belief in one God is the main contribution of Judaism to civilization **14** God determines the fate of all individuals **15** God is totally self-sufficient and does not need man **16** Man cannot improve on what a perfect God has created

ETHICS *More Than Meets the Eye, page 49*

17 Anyone who observes the commandments is defined as a religious Jew **18** Jewish law favors capital punishment **19** Ancient Judaism approved of the institution of slavery **20** Judaism teaches that people are inherently moral **21** All forms of gambling are regarded as sinful **22** Lying is wrong under all circumstances

SEX AND BIRTH *Lesser Known Views, page 67*

23 The offspring of an unmarried couple is regarded as illegitimate **24** Judaism advocates sex for procreation, not for pleasure **25** Jewish law is totally opposed to birth control **26** Judaism makes no allowance for terminating pregnancy **27** A child must be named after a deceased relative **28** A male child is not a Jew until he is circumcised

WOMEN'S ROLE
Varied Opinions, Surprising Responses, page 81

29 A woman may not come in physical contact with a Torah Scroll **30** In Jewish law a woman cannot initiate divorce **31**

DEATH AND MOURNING
Questioning What We Were Told, page 169

SOME COMMON HEBREW EXPRESSIONS
Their Uncommon Meanings, page 193

OPINIONS ABOUT JEWS
Some Common Fallacies, page 207

AFTERWORD, *page 223*

PREFACE

Considering the long history of the Jews, we should not
be surprised that so many myths and misunderstandings
about Judaism have circulated and been handed down
from generation to generation. The process has continued through our own day.

One of the crowning achievements of the Jews was
the *Mishna*, known also as the Oral Law. For centuries
it was verbally studied in the great academies of ancient
Palestine. Eventually the vast material had to be committed to writing to avoid errors that were seeping into
the transmission of these oral laws. Unlike the authoritative Oral Law, a creation of the *tannaim* (sages of the
first to third centuries, C.E.), other "oral traditions"
based on hearsay and popular folklore, were transmitted
from parents to children over the generations. The children were often unaware that their parents were perpetuating misconceptions about Judaism that the parents themselves had inherited. They accepted what they
heard in the home, based on the respectful assumption
that the old knew more about Judaism than the young,
and so these views were not questioned.

With the vast literature available today on topics of
Jewish interest we need not passively accept the distor-
tions others have impressed upon us. Misconceptions,
like myths, do not die easily. They become part of our

emotional makeup. People frequently project what they would like Judaism to say to them because it better fits their personality and mind-set. For example, one who fears dogma in any form may choose to emphasize the rational nature of Judaism, free of all dogma. However, there are several dogmas in Jewish theology that cannot be dismissed merely because we are uncomfortable hearing them. Similarly, people who are forever searching for peace of mind in their personal lives may *want* to feel that the primary goal of their religion is to provide inner peace—an obvious distortion of the prophetic message.

Others, who are apathetic or hostile to religion and who have distanced themselves from Jewish traditions, find the need to reinforce their negative feelings by offering their own brand of misconceptions. They may be sharply critical of what they perceive to be the Jewish view toward capital punishment or the biblical endorsement of slavery. Or they may assume that miracles play a critical role in Jewish belief, as in Christianity, a concept they personally find unacceptable. A hasty generalization helps them to justify their own doubts about the need for religious belief altogether.

Most people who tend to generalize do so because it is convenient. A generalization becomes a useful device for finding the simple answer or solution, the short-cut that helps to avoid closer investigation. You frequently hear that "Jews believe" or "Judaism teaches" as if all Jewish beliefs can be reduced to simple or pat formulas.

But the main sources of Jewish theology—the Talmud, the Midrash, the Prayerbook—include a mosaic of views and attitudes expressed by religious thinkers who often contradict one another.

Some authorities are consistently conservative; others brazenly express thoughts that appear to border on heresy, especially when they humanize God or expound on the origins of man and the universe.

You will not find *the* Jewish belief by discovering a single verse or sentence in an ancient text. The many volumes of the Talmud and *midrashim* are encyclopedic in scope, recording majority and minority views as well as the viewpoint of a lonely individual who could not be ignored by his colleagues. All opinions deserve a hearing and they are faithfully recorded in the sacred texts and studied together. Occasionally the single opinion eventually becomes the accepted belief or practice based on the vast scholarship or the convincing personality of the individual rabbi. But the search for the normative Jewish view on a topic is more often than not elusive and frustrating even for the learned who are familiar with the texts. It is apparent that the ancient rabbis did not concern themselves with formulating a systematic theology nor with catechistic answers to questions of belief. Not until the Middle Ages do we find any attempt to systematize Jewish doctrines.

Another source of confusion among the laity is found in the general attitude about Jewish customs. Many people are unaware of the essential role of the *minhag* or custom in community life. The popular custom of wearing a tie in the office or greeting a friend with a handshake cannot be equated in importance with certain Jewish customs: Unlike such popular customs, many Jewish customs eventually share the same status as a law. In fact, some regional customs became so important that they even took precedence over the prevailing law (*minhag mevattel halakhah*).

Many well-established traditions that are widely accepted in our day started as customs that were practiced by only a cluster of Jews in a small town. In time these customs attracted larger groups and even withstood the opposition of prominent rabbis challenging their value and validity.

Take the *Kol Nidre*, the most widely known part of the service recited on Yom Kippur evening. Few people today would ask that this prayer-formula be abolished even though it is composed of difficult Aramaic words and its content is irrelevant to most worshippers. Yet, the recitation of *Kol Nidre* originated as a custom; it was bitterly opposed as a "foolish custom" by some of the most illustrious *gaonim* (religious leaders of Babylonian Jewry from the end of the sixth to the middle of the eleventh century). The people found a need to retain the *Kol Nidre*, however, and its central role in the service remained.

The Mourner's *kaddish* also began as a custom practiced by a small group. It eventually took hold and evolved into a universally accepted affirmation of faith.

Covering the head on religious occasions was a custom originally limited to Sephardic Jews. Eventually it evolved into a widespread tradition observed by all Jewish males during prayer and Torah study. Then the tradition was extended and the hat or *yarmulke* was worn at all times among the observant, even when they were not performing a sacred act. Not until the advent of Reform Judaism in the nineteenth century was the propriety of wearing a head covering challenged by a segment of the community. Thus, to speak of a Jewish practice as "mere" custom based on its origin does not take into account the essential role of the *minhag* in the daily life of the Jewish community. The will of the people persisted.

A reminder. We cannot always be guided by the origin of a Jewish practice to determine its validity in our day. Some laws clearly originated in superstition, yet they continue to be widely observed. We may reject the original reasons for their observance without discarding those practices which long ago were incorporated into the rubric of Jewish law. In observing them we are not being asked to compromise our intellectual honesty by perpetuating superstitious beliefs.

One of many examples: At one time the Mourner's *kaddish* was recited for an entire year since it was felt that the memory of the departed remained vivid for twelve months. However, since twelve months was also regarded as the maximum period of punishment for the wicked in the heavenly court, the recitation of *kaddish* for a whole year might imply that the son felt his parent deserved the maximum penalty. Therefore, the period of recitation of the *kaddish* was reduced by one month, and we continue to recite it for eleven months although the original reason for its observance has long faded into oblivion. The redeeming value of retaining the observance remains: It helps to strengthen the emotional ties between the mourner and other worshippers in the synagogue during the crucial months of bereavement.

Because the contemporary rabbi is constantly engaging in dialogue with the laity, he is in the unique position of hearing attitudes and opinions about Jews and Judaism. He receives feedback in the classroom; reactions after a sermon; responses after a lecture or after a funeral. At the house of mourning people offer opinions and observations about death and the dying; during a counseling session he becomes privy to the most candid impressions concerning religion; at an informal social gathering the discussion occasionally turns to topics of

Jewish interest where opinions are freely exchanged and the rabbi's response is solicited.

Over the years I have been intrigued by these attitudes and opinions, especially the myths and misconceptions that our people cling to. Where did they originate? How have these misconceptions affected the people who continue believing in them? Would their commitment to Judaism have been different were their assumptions corrected earlier in their lives?

The rich variety of expressions about Jewish beliefs and practices found in this volume have all been voiced by laymen with whom I have had contact over many years. I decided to record their views with the goal of presenting more appropriate views of Judaism.

Unfortunately, I never had the opportunity to respond personally to all the people who expressed the opinions and attitudes covered in this volume. This book represents a modest but conscientious attempt to reach those who are receptive to second thoughts about Judaism.

Especially in the area of Jewish beliefs, I recognize the difficulty of remaining objective in my responses, although I have attempted to avoid the temptation to sermonize. Rather I have tried to capture the essence of what I believe expresses the normative or classical Jewish view, even though I cannot always agree with it on a personal level.

Anyone who motivates a teacher to continue with his studies is worthy of being called a colleague. The men, women,* and children who have challenged me to

---

* I would have preferred employing inclusive terms in writing, rather than using male terminology. However, the inadequacy of the English language and the cumbersome he/she, him/her alternative, left me little choice but, regretfully, to follow the old usage.

continue exploring Jewish sources are all true colleagues. They have earned my profound gratitude and respect.

Acknowledgments

I am most fortunate to find colleagues who are also faithful friends. When I asked them to read this material and to be candid with their reactions, they did not hesitate to read it carefully and to criticize freely. I wish to express my gratitude especially to Rabbis Jules Harlow, Andre Ungar and Bernard Zlotowitz who offered me so many suggestions for the improvement of this volume. Lippman Bodoff with his keen eye for detail and his vast knowledge of Jewish sources has been a most valuable critic.

I wish that I could personally thank Rachel Rabinowicz, of blessed memory, who carefully read this manuscript in its initial stages and encouraged me with her little notes urging me to continue my writing. Ilene McGrath has earned my respect and admiration for her editing skills. Selma Herman, my devoted secretary at the Fair Lawn Jewish Center, typed this material "the old-fashioned way," always with her personal and caring touch. Edith Sobel along with her many literary talents helped me immeasurably by typing the entire book on her word processor.

I am indebted to my friends Jacob Behrman and Adam Bengal with whom I have worked so closely in preparing this material for publication.

BASIC BELIEFS
What Jews Really Believe

1 The Jews constitute a race

In the pre-Nazi period Jews were frequently referred to as a race by both their friends and adversaries as well as by Jews themselves. Those who spoke of the Jewish race in a complimentary way did not take the trouble to examine the implications of attributing racial characteristics to Jews. Many anti-Semites, on the other hand, spoke deliberately of the Jewish race because they believed that all Jews possessed certain genetic qualities — physical, mental and characterological — that set them apart from others; these inherited qualities were considered a threat to the decent elements in their society.

Hitler and his propagandists further exploited the racial theory in regard to Jews. It made sense to attribute inherent characteristics to *all* Jews. As a race they possessed inferior Jewish "blood." All contact between them and the Germans had to be terminated in order to avoid contamination of the German master race. In September 1935 the Nuremberg Racial Laws were promulgated in order to preserve the racial purity of the Nazis. Anyone possessing more than one-quarter Jewish "blood" in his veins was not to be regarded German and was to be removed from German national life, a demonic concept that led to the eventual extermination of one-third of world Jewry.

No scientific evidence can be found to show that the Jews constitute a race. The genetic differences between Jews in one country and Jews in another can be as great as those between the non-Jews of the same two countries. Furthermore, the genetic characteristics of every Jewish group in the Diaspora strongly resembles those of non-Jews among whom the Jews have lived. One does not have to be an anthropologist to observe the striking physical differences among Jews who have come to Israel from Germany and those from Morocco, from Yemen and from Ethiopia. They are all Jews in spite of the diversity of their physical characteristics.

The familiar game of trying to determine "who looks Jewish?" in a social gathering or the usually complimentary observation that "you don't look Jewish!" cannot be verified in light of our present knowledge about the variety of physical features among Jews.

2 Judaism is a religion

It is difficult for some people to conceive of Judaism other than as a religion, one of the major religions of mankind. Judaism has often been called the mother religion to Christianity and Islam. In America Judaism has long been considered one of the three major religious groups, along with Catholicism and Protestantism. When asked to fill in one's religion on a questionnaire, we usually respond: Jewish.

Judaism, however, is not synonymous with the religion of the Jew. In fact, there is no word for religion in biblical Hebrew. There is the word *emunah*, which means faith or faithfulness, but not religion. Also in the later books of the Bible there is found the term *dat*, denoting custom, law or usage, but not religion. When the groom places the ring on the bride's finger, he utters the words "*kedat moshe veyisrael*," which does not refer to the broad term religion but rather to the law required by Moses and Israel. Dr. Louis Finkelstein has observed that "The most deeply religious of men had no word for religion."

Judaism embraces much more than the religion of the Jew, though religion is an integral part of Judaism. In addition, Judaism includes the whole civilization of the Jewish people—its history, cultural experience, ethical system, language, identification with the land and people of Israel, etc. These are all vital areas embraced by the term Judaism. Mordecai M. Kaplan elaborated on this broad definition of Judaism in his classic, *Judaism as a Civilization*.

Since Judaism is more than the religion of the Jew, we can understand why a secular Jew who promotes Jewish culture or the principles of Zionism may still contribute to the enhancement of Judaism. He is still identified as a Jew.

Although their numbers have dwindled in recent years, many non-religious Jews who originated in Eastern Europe enjoyed a vibrant Jewish cultural life; they were Yiddish devotees and contributed to its rich literature, promoted the Jewish arts, and were unyielding in their commitment to Jewish survival.

Occasionally conflicts arose between ethnic Jews and the religious Jewish community. Yet, no religious Jew questioned whether the secularist should be regarded as a Jew. Since Judaism encompassed more than religion, the non-religious Jew was regarded as authentic, albeit misdirected.

3 Belief in miracles is essential to the Jewish faith

A miracle is usually understood as an event that is a suspension of the law of nature. Many Jews accept the belief in miracles as essential to Judaism. Their religious faith leads them to accept God's ability to change the natural order. A religion without supernatural intervention leaves no room for faith.

Yet, belief in supernatural miracles plays a relatively minor role in Jewish theology, in contrast to Christianity. For example, the belief that Moses was the greatest prophet and teacher in Jewish history did not depend on his performing miraculous demonstrations to prove his special relationship with God.

The Torah does mention several miraculous events that took place, especially during the forty years in the wilderness—the manna, the earth that opened up to devour Korah and his followers, Balaam's donkey that spoke to his master. The Mishna does not gloss over these and other miracles described in the Torah. It is apparent that the early rabbis in the Mishnaic Era were troubled by the thought that God would interfere with the order of nature to create miracles. These events were explained in the following way: When He formed the world, God created several miracles at twilight just before the first Sabbath. God created these special events at the time of creation to be used in the future when they would be needed. In providing a special creation God did not have to disturb the laws of nature in the future.

Another method of explaining the miracles in the Bible was to allegorize them. In the Book of Exodus the Israelites waged war against the Amalekites. The text reads: "And when Moses held up his hand, Israel prevailed; when he let down his hand, Amalek prevailed" (Exod. 17:11). The obvious question is asked in the Talmud: "Could the hands of Moses make the battle or break the battle?" The rabbis explained that this physical gesture by Moses had only symbolic significance. For as long as the Israelites looked upward and kept their hearts in submission to their Father in Heaven, they prevailed; otherwise they were defeated. The presence of Moses gave the Israelites courage to fight against the enemy.

The Jewish philosophers, and especially Maimonides, were sensitive to the problem of accepting miracles as literal truth. Maimonides believed that the miracles attributed to the prophets did not literally take place as actual events but occurred in their "prophetic vision." This is how the philosopher interpreted Jacob's wrestling with an angel before meeting with his brother Esau (Gen. 32:25). Therefore, by calling these miracles "prophetic visions" rather than actual events, Maimonides was able to maintain his belief that Judaism does not defy the laws of science and reason.

The Mishna states that a prayer requesting God to change events that have already occurred is a meaningless prayer. Thus,

> If his wife was pregnant and he said, "May it be Your will that my wife give birth to a male," this is

an empty prayer. If he was returning from a journey and heard a sound of lament in the city, and he said, "May it be Your will that those who lament not be of my household," his prayer is in vain" (Berakhot 9:3).

How can one pray that God change his predicament after it has already occurred? God would be interfering with the natural order.

The foremost sages maintained that miracles cannot be invoked to support one's views. The Talmud records a legendary story about Rabbi Eliezer who was unable to convince his colleagues that his opinion was correct. He performed a number of spectacular events to sway them to his side but without success. When a carob tree was miraculously moved a hundred yards from its place in support of Rabbi Eliezer's opinion, his colleagues answered, "We do not derive proof from a carob tree." Eliezer then caused the water to flow backwards and the walls of the school to incline. Even a heavenly voice proclaimed Eliezer to be correct. But the sages were still not impressed. And so Rabbi Jeremiah boldly declared, "The Torah was given to us on Mount Sinai, so we do not pay attention to a Heavenly voice." Rabbi Jeremiah was saying in effect that we reject miracles to prove the correctness of an interpretation of the Torah. We rely instead on the majority decision of the rabbinic authorities.

Miracles then are certainly mentioned as having occurred throughout the sacred literature. But Judaism does not depend on belief in these miracles as a requirement of loyalty to the Jewish faith. Miracles can be reinterpreted or allegorized without compromising one's commitment to Judaism.

Although the word *miracle* literally implies the suspension of nature's laws, it is frequently used more loosely to describe unexpected or unusual phenomena rather than supernatural interference with the law of nature. For example, the continued existence of the Jewish people against all odds and the reemergence of the State of Israel after two millenia of Jewish homelessness are often referred to as miracles although these achievements did not require God's suspending the physical laws of the universe.

4 Unlike Christians, Jews were never required to accept dogmas

We generally understand a dogma to be a tenet or doctrine which has the support of a central authority such as the Church. For example, belief in the Trinity or the Virgin Birth is accepted as a dogma among devout Catholics throughout the world.

Among Jews there has never been a central authority to proclaim dogmas that all Jews were required to follow. For centuries many Jewish thinkers differentiated Judaism from Christianity by asserting that Judaism contains no dogmas. Moses Mendelsohn, the German Jewish philosopher, was a leading exponent of the absence of dogma in Judaism. He believed that Judaism was primarily a rational religion and that reason and dogma were incompatible. Judaism would not require its adherents to accept a doctrine merely on faith, he held, especially if it defied reason.

Almost no one challenged Mendelsohn's view until Solomon Schechter, who became the head of the Jewish Theological Seminary, wrote an essay on the "Dogmas of Judaism." Schechter was fully aware that there was no single authority that proclaimed Jewish dogmas, but he contended that Judaism does contain doctrines of faith. "It (Judaism) regulates not only our actions but also our thoughts. We usually urge that in Judaism religion means life; but we forget that a life without guiding principles is a life not worth living."

It is generally agreed that the Hebrew Bible does not contain dogmas. The Talmud as well does not dwell on formulating dogmas that Jews were required to follow. Yet, we do find in the Mishna Sanhedrin the beginnings of a Creed for Jews to follow:

"These are excluded from the world to come: (1) One who says there is no resurrection after death. (2) One who denies that the Torah is divine. (3) The *epikoros*." There are conflicting views as to the meaning of *epikoros*. Some say this refers to a person who denies belief in reward and punishment. Others regard him as one who denies tradition. Schechter claims that it refers to one who treats the words of Scripture or tradition in a frivolous way.

It was not until the Middle Ages that serious attempts were made to establish a creed for all Jews to follow. Jews at that time were being challenged by Greek philosophy, Christianity and Islam, and so it became crucial to define Jewish belief and its uniqueness.

The best known Creed was formulated by Moses Maimonides (1135-1204), who composed the "Thirteen Articles of Faith" found in his commentary to the Mishna. His creed included some of the following principles of faith: The existence of God, the eternity of God; belief in prophecy; belief that the Torah cannot be changed; the coming of the Messiah. Maimonides contended that without adhering to specific beliefs a Jew could not attain immortality. The unbeliever was to be excluded from the Jewish people.

The thirteen principles of Maimonides were accepted by the majority of Jews and eventually inserted with some variation into most traditional prayer books.

Each article of faith was also introduced by the formal phrase, *ani maamin* — "I believe" — which was intended to establish the thirteen principles as an authoritative creed. For the first time an attempt was made to introduce dogmas into Judaism in order to encourage correct beliefs alongside the commandments requiring action, such as Sabbath and holiday observance.

Although Maimonides was widely accepted, his thirteen principles were opposed by some scholars, who were against reducing the principles of Judaism to thirteen. Others chose different basic principles.

In our day we would find it difficult to ask any Jew to conform to a loyalty test based on a set of dogmas, and for several reasons: First, we have no central power which speaks with authority for world Jewry. Second, most contemporary Jews would not accept the proposition that uniform belief is essential to remaining an authentic Jew. Yet, we cannot dismiss the effort to introduce dogma into Judaism by the foremost theologians of the Middle Ages. They were responding to a need: To preserve the uniqueness of Jewish beliefs in face of the serious challenges to Judaism by Christianity and Islam.

5   The main function of the Hebrew prophets was to predict the future

Most dictionaries associate the words *prophet* and *prophecy* with the ability to predict future events; the words are derived from the Greek *prophetes* ("to speak before"). Since the Hebrew word *navi* is usually translated as "prophet," it is just assumed that the primary role of the Hebrew prophets was also to tell the future in the same tradition as the ancient Greek prophecies.

This popular definition when applied to the Hebrew prophets is inaccurate for it does not convey the primary function of the *navi*, who was a human "spokesman" or "mouthpiece" for God. In the Book of Exodus God reassures the reluctant Moses : "See, I make you an oracle to Pharaoh, and your brother Aaron shall be your *spokesman* (*neviekha*)." The prophet, then, speaks forth on God's behalf.

It is true that the prophet was also called *hozeh* or *ro-eh*, both meaning "a seer." It is generally believed that among the ancient Hebrews there existed soothsayers and fortune tellers who plied their trade even during the age of the great prophets of Israel. Occasionally these genuine prophets would use some of the same primitive devices to induce religious ecstasy, such as producing a sign to show that their message was true. Beginning around the eighth century B.C.E., however, the classical prophets distanced themselves from the sooth-sayers and their methods. They became convinced that the substance of their prophecy did not require the support of magic or trances.

When the Hebrew prophets did venture a prediction, it was usually a conditional prognosis. Prophetic passages that predict national destruction or exile may yet be avoided by a change in direction to God and away from idolatry, pride, or excessive materialism. The key word in predictive prophecies is "if" — *if* you will obey the Lord, then your people will be amply rewarded; *if* you will not hearken to Him, then know that these will be the destructive consequences of disobedience.

As a spokesman for God, the prophet revealed to his people or to the adversary what God wanted him to say. The true prophet was never a professional for hire nor did he affiliate with another group of prophets. He stood alone. He was usually reluctant to accept God's calling to become a prophet. He would question his own maturity, his fluency, his moral fitness. But God perceived more about him and his abilities than the prophet knew about himself. Once he embarked on his special calling, he became so imbued with God's spirit that he could not compromise his ideals, his passion for justice.

Ahad Ha-Am in his classical essay on "Priest and Prophet" concedes that other nations produced prophets at various times, "but it is pre-eminently among the ancient Hebrews that prophecy is found. ... Prophecy is, as it were, the hallmark of the Hebrew national spirit."

6   Saints have no place in Jewish thought

Contemporary Jews rarely refer to individuals as saints, no matter what their moral achievement or personal piety. There's a reason for this reluctance, for usually a saint refers to a person of exceptional holiness, formally canonized by the Catholic Church.

Although Jews did not elevate their co-religionists into official sainthood, however, they did speak of the saintliness of exceptional individuals. People of rare virtue and benevolence were at one time referred to as saints.

The rabbis in the Mishna discuss the special virtues of the *hasid*, usually translated as saint. They place the *hasid* highest on the scale of virtue because he goes beyond the mere observance of the law. He does not wait until he is asked to perform a commandment. Also, the *hasid* says, "Mine is thine and thine is thine." Further, he is "hard to anger and easy to pacify."

The *hasid* is not satisfied to wait until the appointed time for prayer. Because of his religious enthusiasm, he prepares for congregational worship with serious deliberation and individual prayer before the service. He continues to pray long after the other worshippers have fulfilled their religious duty.

The Jewish saint delights in exercising self-discipline. He consciously controls his speech and measures his words. He does not permit himself the luxury of overeating or excessive drinking lest he degrade himself to the animal level.

Most important on his scale of values, the *hasid* seeks to draw closer to all God's creation — Jew and non-Jew, friend and foe, human being and beast. We find the credo of the *hasid* in the *Little Book of Saints*:

> Refrain your kindness and compassion from nothing which the Holy One, blessed be He, created in this world. Never beat or inflict pain on any animal, beast, bird or insect; nor throw stones at a dog or cat; nor kill flies or wasps.

Dr. Louis Ginzberg, former Professor of Talmud at the Jewish Theological Seminary, in his book *Students, Scholars and Saints*, defines saintliness as "only another word for heroism in the domain of ethics and religion." He is impressed by the famous French critic, Sainte Beuve, who describes the heroism of the Saint "as an inner state which above all is one of love and humility, of infinite confidence in God, and of strictness toward one's self accompanied with tenderness for others."

Ginzberg dedicates an entire essay in his volume to Rabbi Israel Salanter (1816-1909), the great scholar and moralist who best personifies the ideal of the Jewish saint. Salanter's life represents all saintly personalities known for their "purity, asceticism and charity."

Purity. The saint serves God without expecting reward for his service. Though he believes in the principle of Reward and Punishment, he is motivated to act morally purely out of love of God, nothing more.

Asceticism. Although Judaism does not encourage the ascetic who resorts to self-punishment or escape from the community, Salanter lived a most frugal life. His material needs were minimal. At times he would refrain from conversation for long periods for he detested small talk and engaged in it only when he felt that he could elevate the spirits of a depressed person.

Charity. Although Salanter had almost no material possessions to distribute to the poor, he gave of himself to those whom he could help. No matter how severe the weather, he would go from house to house to solicit help for those in need. He always had concern for the sensibilities of the poor, never permitting himself to embarrass them.

Israel Salanter would also act charitably to those who wronged him. He would seek every opportunity to show some kindness even to those who injured him just as God shows kindness to the sinner.

Admittedly, only a small segment of the community could attain the rare moral qualities of the Jewish saint. In fact, most contemporaries would not even want to be identified with saintliness, which requires excessive self-discipline and sacrifice. Yet, one cannot help but acknowledge those few individualists in every age who defy convention in order to achieve a higher degree of spirituality.

7   Belief in the Chosen People implies superiority over other peoples

The belief that the Jewish people have a special relationship with God is one of the basic doctrines of Judaism. The origin of this unique relationship between God and Israel is originally expressed in the Book of Exodus:

> Now then, if you will obey Me faithfully and keep My covenant, you shall be My treasured possession among all the peoples. Indeed, all the earth is Mine, but you shall be to Me a kingdom of priests and a holy nation.

Similar pronouncements are also found in the writings of the prophets. The Jewish Prayerbook reaffirms this belief in Israel's special relationship with God: "You have chosen us among all the nations; you have loved us and favored us." The Jew expresses this same principle of Israel's chosenness in the words of the blessing he recites when he is called to the Torah (that is, called up for an *aliyah*).

Through the ages many non-Jews sharply criticized what appeared to them a claim to national or racial superiority. If God is Creator of all peoples, should they not be equally precious to Him? There is no doubt that the Jewish belief in their chosenness has contributed to resentment, and even to open hostility against the Jewish people.

Some sensitive Jews as well have argued that this exclusive concept has become obsolete and should no longer be included in the Jewish liturgy. For example, Professor Mordecai Kaplan, who contributed so much to the enrichment of Jewish ideas and institutions, removed all references to the Chosen People in the prayerbook that he edited. The debate in Jewish circles over the validity of this basic principle of Jewish belief continues.

It should be understood, however, that to affirm that the Jews are God's chosen people never implied that they were free to exploit other peoples or to regard themselves as God's elite corps to be ensured His protection regardless of their behavior. The doctrine of election implied merely a serious responsibility to uphold the moral law. Failure to live up to God's moral requirements of His people could count more heavily against them than against those who were not elected. The prophet Amos (eighth cent. B.C.E.) dispelled any notions of God's favored treatment toward the Israelites when he declared: "You alone have I singled out of all the families of the earth; that is why I will call you to account for all your iniquities."

To be chosen from among all the peoples was never intended to confer feelings of superiority over others. The Israelites had agreed to become a unique people in choosing to accept the Torah when God offered it to them in the wilderness. Uniqueness does not imply genetic superiority, however. Neither is the religion of the Jews considered the only true or valid religion. The Jewish people was not called upon by God to convert the world to the only "true" faith, implying that all other faiths are false. If this were the basic meaning of chosenness, then it would certainly be difficult to continue teaching this essential concept of Jewish belief.

The Bible refers to the unique status of the Israelites by calling them *am kadosh* and *goy kadosh* (holy people and holy nation). The word for marriage, *kiddushin*, derives from the same word *kadosh*. After the marriage ceremony, husband and wife enjoy a sacred relationship, yet they are not expected to feel superior to other women or men. By the same token, a sacred relationship was formed at Mount Sinai between the Israelite people and God. This unique relationship does not imply that other groups are in any way inferior. All individuals and groups may enjoy access to God.

8   Belief in a Satan
was always alien to Judaism

We cannot simply ignore the many references to Satan in Jewish sources merely because most Jews do not believe in his existence today. The *hashkivenu* prayer recited every evening of the year refers to Satan, usually translated freely as adversary or temptation. In the morning prayers as well the worshipper asks to be spared from "The Satan who corrupts." On the High Holy Days the Cantor requests God to "rebuke the Satan so that he does not accuse me."

The Satan is mentioned in several biblical passages, usually appearing as a common noun referring to the enemy who obstructs and opposes. In later biblical sources the proper noun "Satan," a familiar character, is found. For example, in the Books of Zechariah and Job, Satan acts as a prosecutor in God's court.

In the Talmud Satan is referred to as an impersonal force, not a specific personality. He is the tempter, the accuser — rarely an independent personality. A common folk saying taken from the Talmud is, "Do not open your mouth to Satan." This expression warns us against uttering a statement that would invite Satan to step in and perform his mischief. Jumping to admit guilt prematurely, or exaggerating our own faults is an invitation to the Satan to exploit our lack of self-esteem.

One of the reasons given for sounding the Shofar on Rosh Hashanah is to "confuse the Satan." Yom Kippur is the only day of the year when Satan has no power. The numerical equivalent of Satan in the Hebrew language adds up to 364, suggesting that only on one day of the year, Yom Kippur, he cannot penetrate the solid ranks of the Jewish people.

With all the references to Satan in the Bible, the Talmud, and liturgy, Satan is never God's equal or rival; he cannot act without permission from God. Satan plays no essential role in Jewish theology such as he assumes in classical Christian belief, in which he possesses divine or demonic power and struggles against God for supremacy. Nowhere in Judaism is Satan pictured as the creator of evil, or as possessing power over death. Most significant, Satan has no power over the soul of man, no ability to deprive him of his freedom. By contrast, in the Gospels Satan becomes the embodiment of the spirit of evil as an independent personality, the Anti-Christ. He is the author of all evil (Luke 10:19).

Jewish theologian Kaufmann Kohler observed that the Jewish view of Satan along with evil spirits remained a matter of popular belief but "never became a positive doctrine of the Synagogue." This view partially explains why the Jewish masses up until the modern period would often refer to the destructiveness of Satan without accepting his existence as a condition of their faith in Judaism. Satan was more of a poetic figure than a literal presence in their lives.

Most contemporary Jews, both traditional and nontraditional, seldom refer to Satan as a force to contend with in their personal lives. Even theologians who have desperately attempted to find some meaning to the tragedy of the Holocaust do not refer to the influence of

Satan as the agent of evil. There are no facile explanations to such an unprecedented tragedy that can adequately explain the destruction of six million Jews. By attributing responsibility to Satan, we would be denying the importance of free will and *human* responsibility.

One of the contributing factors culminating in the Holocaust was the medieval Christian doctrine that Jews were the "spawn of Satan." For centuries Jews were identified with the Satan. They were accused of being sorcerers, magicians — a sub-human species. This theory continued to be held by German anti-Semites in the nineteenth and twentieth centuries and was adopted by Nazi propagandists as a valid reason for extirpating the Jewish people.

Although the vast majority of Jews do not accept the influence of a Satan in the literal sense, the term is still used allegorically to express temptation or a destructive impulse within a person whose sudden change of behavior defies understanding.

9 Judaism completely rejects the monastic or ascetic life

What is meant by the monastic or ascetic life? Succinctly, it means a retreat to the self and away from society. Monasticism can take on different forms such as the refusal to marry and bear children for the future. It may include frequent fasting as a form of self-purification. In the extreme form, certain monastics would punish their bodies by self-flagellation.

Generally speaking, Judaism frowns upon the ascetic or monastic life. Most *mitzvot* are performed in the presence of others in the family or in participation with the larger community. The commandment to be fruitful and multiply, the first one mentioned in the Bible, is so essential to Judaism that the requirement to marry and bear children has always been taken with utmost seriousness by traditional Jews.

Not a single one of the 613 commandments—positive or negative—requires any form of asceticism or punishment of the body. Even the command to fast on Yom Kippur was never intended to inflict pain on the body. The discomfort that accompanies self-denial on Yom Kippur does not imply that physical pain should be felt.

Scholars have frequently pointed out that the Jewish attitude toward monasticism constitutes one of the great differences between early Judaism and Christianity. Paul for example, was a celibate. Furthermore, speaking of his celibacy, Paul said, "Would that all men were as I." To Paul, the marriage relationship between a man and a woman was a concession to the flesh. It is better to marry than to burn, he conceded, but the single life was preferable.

Søren Kierkegaard was a strong proponent of Pauline Christianity. He renounced the state of marriage and said that man should seek a life of solitude and isolation. Above all, according to Kierkegaard, he should suffer. For a year and a half he practiced total asceticism "to see how much I could bear." Kierkegaard declared, "Back to the cloister. There is only one thing higher, and that is martyrdom."

This view of early Christianity was denounced by Martin Luther in his reformation. To this day a number of Catholics find their highest form of religious expression by living in monasteries isolated from the general community. Some practice silence most of the day and abstain from those pleasures that we regard as normal.

Monasticism was not an alien idea to all Jews in their long history, however. Although it was never practiced by sizable numbers, it was idealized by clusters of Jews and was advocated by some well-known Jewish philosophers such as Abraham ibn Hiyya, who advocated sexual abstinence as the ideal.

We still have incomplete information about the sect called Essenes. Philo, the historian-philosopher, records that the Essenes rejected marriage and that there were no youths among them. The Qumran sect whose writings were discovered near the Dead Sea were probably Essenes. Its members lived together and shared all things communally. They fled the large cities and lived an isolated life with the belief that the world was soon coming to an end. The rabbis mentioned still other groups who lived monastic lives. They were called Silent Ones (*Hashaim*), Humble Ones (*Anavim*), and Chaste Ones (*Tzenuim*). Little is known about these Jewish sects.

Although the guiding principle of Hillel to avoid separation from the community was generally accepted by the rabbis, there were exceptions. For example, Ben Azzai did not marry. When he was criticized by his colleagues for living the single life, he responded: "What can I do? My soul is in love with the Torah. The world will have to be populated by others." What is significant here is that Ben Azzai felt compelled to justify his actions before his rabbinic colleagues.

Another classical source from the Mishna supporting the monastic view is found in *Ethics of the Fathers* (*Pirke Avot*):

This is the life style for students of Torah: Eat a salty crust of bread, ration your drinking water, live a life of privation, exhaust yourself in Torah study. If you will live in this manner, "you will be happy and all will go well with you." "You will be happy" in this world; "All will go well with you" in the world-to-come.

Monasticism tends to arise among a small minority of Jews after a national catastrophe. Following the Crusades, which destroyed hundreds of Jewish communities, there appeared a small group of Jewish mystics with ascetic tendencies. Their mentor was Judah The Pious, who in the twelfth or thirteenth century wrote *Sefer Hasidim*, a book whose dominant theme was that the truly pious should forsake this world. It declared that one should reduce to a minimum his conversation with men, young and old, even with his wife. He should not even take a walk for pleasure. He should rather engage in rigorous forms of penitential acts. The foremost authority of Jewish mysticism Gershom Scholem described the regimen of these extreme ascetics:

> To sit in the snow or on the ice for an hour daily in winter, or to expose one's body to ants and bees in the summer was a common practice among those who followed the new call.

This sect was probably very limited and did not capture the imagination of the vast majority of Jews, even among the survivors of the Crusades; most of them began rebuilding their communities, giving birth to large families and attempting to find joy in the Sabbaths and holidays. It is amazing how rapidly they replenished their losses.

In answer to the question whether Jews rejected the monastic life altogether, the response must be negative. Monastics were never expelled or excommunicated for voluntarily isolating themselves from the Jewish community or for renouncing marriage, even though they removed themselves from the mainstream of Jewish life and thought.

Rav, who established a great academy in Babylonia, expressed the more acceptable Jewish view: "A man will some day have to give an account to God for all the good things which his eyes beheld and of which he refused to partake." He also said to his student: "My son, live according to your ability, do good to yourself, for there is no enjoyment in the nether world, nor will death be long in coming."

10 Judaism discourages controversy and debate

Although seeking peace is regarded as the greatest of virtues, controversy should not be ignored as an integral part of Judaism. The whole Talmudic tradition contains records of arguments and controversies among prominent scholars. In fact, one cannot properly appreciate Judaism without examining the heated debates about Jewish law. Jews more than any other group have thrived on the principle that argumentation can elicit the highest qualities in people.

A distinction should be made here between an argument and a quarrel. When we argue, we challenge the next person to persuade us that his view is more convincing. When we quarrel, we are not generally receptive to the other person's views. We are not listening to him, but only to ourselves.

The Mishna differentiates between positive and destructive controversies: "Every controversy which is for the sake of Heaven (spiritually motivated) will endure in the end, but one which is not for the sake of Heaven will not endure." Then follows examples of the two kinds of controversy: Hillel and Shammai, the foremost representatives of two great schools of thought, often debated with each other, but both endeavored to achieve the same end—the enhancement of religious values. They differed primarily in their interpretation of the law. On the other hand, when Korah argued with Moses, his motives were personal and self-centered. He sought to uproot Moses' authority and elevate himself in Moses' stead. Korah entered into controversy which was "not for the sake of Heaven," a destructive act.

After the death of Hillel and Shammai their students continued to dispute each other on ritual and theological questions alike. The Talmud Eruvin records that for two and a half years the Schools of Shammai and Hillel disputed each other. The School of Shammai argued that it would have been better for man not to have been created; the School of Hillel argued that it was better for man to have been created than not. In the end, a vote was taken, and it was decided: "It would have been better for man not to have been created, but now that He is created, let him examine his deeds."

Most of the debates between the great rabbis are faithfully preserved in the Talmud. Rabban Gamliel vs. Rabbi Eliezer; Rabbi Akiba vs. Rabbi Ishmael; Rav vs. Samuel. Often we find one prominent Rabbi who debates alone against the majority. The single opinion was usually overruled but that did not deter the dissenter from vigorously expressing his view. And these debates are recorded so future generations of students can review all sides of the argument.

A revealing discussion is found in the Talmud (Bava Metzia, 59b) between Rabbi Eliezer and his colleagues. They were debating a detail of ritual cleanliness. Rabbi Eliezer's opinion differed from the view of all the other scholars, yet he persisted in his interpretation by asking that a series of miracles appear to prove that he was correct. Although miracles allegedly occurred at his behest, Eliezer's colleagues were not moved. Finally, Eliezer appealed to heaven itself and a heavenly voice declared that Eliezer was correct.

Then Rabbi Joshua stood up and quoted from Deuteronomy (30:12), "The Law is not in heaven." Rabbi Jeremiah explained the meaning of this verse quoted by Rabbi Joshua: Once the Israelites accepted the Torah on Sinai, the Law [Torah] was given into the hands of people and the collective judgment of the Sages must be relied upon to interpret the law.

Rabbi Nathan, who was listening intently to the debate, met Elijah the prophet. Nathan asked him, "What was the Holy One, Blessed be He, doing in that hour?"

Elijah responded, "God was laughing and saying, 'My children have defeated Me, my children have defeated Me.'"

This extraordinary story reveals a uniquely Jewish approach: God is delighted and impressed when He listens to the sharp debate among His children. The text implies that God desires his children to debate theological issues. It is as if God were saying, "You have overwhelmed Me with your keen powers of reasoning. Keep up the good work."

This spirit of controversy continued unabated throughout the Middle Ages as well. The Gaonim, religious leaders of Babylonian Jewry, would often lock horns in debating interpretation of Jewish law. Saadya Gaon, with his towering intellect, accepted the challenge of the Karaites, who were the religious fundamentalists of their day. After Maimonides died, his defenders argued vehemently with his adversaries, the anti-Maimunists.

To this very day, controversy continues to take place in Jewish life both in Israel and in the Diaspora. The debate over "Who is a Jew?" constantly reverberates in the halls of the Knesset, not to speak of other sharp debates among the political parties in Israel. In America the issues of women's rights in the Synagogue and the admission of women into the rabbinate have been passionately debated by scholars and laymen alike. And most recently, controversy surrounding patrilineal descent has divided the Jewish community.

The claim that Jews have been an argumentative people is a mild understatement, but they are the inheritors of an intellectual heritage that has invited debate. Contemporary Jews have been shaped by their history, and they need not feel defensive about their passion for debate.

Naturally, Jews pay a price for their controversial nature: At times they may choose to argue just for the sake of argument. They consider it their right to debate even inconsequential issues or merely to play the devil's advocate. They are reluctant to accept group discipline, even when such discipline is vital to a unified Jewish community. But the rewards have also been beneficial. "When scholars compete, wisdom gains." The urge to debate issues has helped Jews to keep their minds active and to achieve even higher levels of creativity. Jewish concern in the areas of politics and social reform has been influenced by their training in debate and argument over the centuries.

11 The theory of Evolution is incompatible with Jewish thought

Many Jewish students who receive religious instruction in their early years never participate in a candid discussion on the question of whether the evolutionary theory of creation is compatible with Jewish thought. These children usually enter adulthood *assuming* that the biblical version of creation is totally incompatible with the generally accepted theory that man evolved from the simplest forms of life over a period of millions of years. This assumption that Judaism is antagonistic to scientific discovery has been known to discourage further study of Jewish sources on an adult level.

Those who further examine the basic Jewish attitude to the Bible may find two views operating together: First, acceptance on faith that the Bible is the inspired work of God; second, the freedom to interpret the biblical text in light of new theories discovered by later generations. By accepting both attitudes simultaneously, Jews remained faithful to their sacred Torah yet were not bound to the literal interpretation of the Bible.

The scholars in the Talmudic period felt free to suggest some daring observations about the origins of man and the universe without violating the spirit of the Torah. Rabbi Judah observed that man was first created with a tail like an animal, but God removed this tail from him to preserve his dignity. Another view: Up until the generation of Enosh, grandson of Adam, the faces of people resembled those of monkeys (the biblical name Enosh connotes a civilized person). A theory about the origin of the universe: God shot a stone over the waters, and from this shooting stone the earth was formed.

These rabbinic observations do not imply that Darwin suggested nothing new or that the ancient rabbis were also scientists. They do indicate, however, that the ancient teachers of Judaism did not look upon the biblical version as a complete statement about the universe. The rabbis did not refrain from speculation. They felt free to fill in the gaps in the biblical version of creation without compromising their reverence for the God-inspired text of the Torah.

The Torah was never intended to serve as a textbook of scientific facts. It is rather a textbook of morality, teaching man how to live in harmony with God's ethical requirements. *The Hebrew Bible concerns itself with eternal truths and not scientific facts.*

Can the traditionalist Jew then accept the theory of evolution or some future scientific discovery that may never have been anticipated in the Bible? Yes, provided he accepts the belief that man did not evolve by mere accident; God was and remains responsible for the creative process.

Whether man was created as described in Genesis or whether he slowly evolved over millions of years is not of vital importance. What is essential is that man was created in God's spiritual image, that he is qualitatively different from the animal kingdom, and that all mankind is related since we allegedly stem from one father and mother, the biblical Adam and Eve.

12 The main goal of religious belief is to provide peace of mind

In 1946 Rabbi Joshua Loth Liebman wrote *Peace of Mind*, which earned instant popularity and remained at the top of the best-seller list for many months. Liebman attempted to show how the goals of psychology and religion complement each other. Together they provide the emotional tranquility that eludes most people. After Liebman's successful book, a spate of books and articles appeared also emphasizing that the primary function of religion is to calm man's troubled soul.

In more recent years other talented Jewish writers have taken exception to the comfortable theory proposed by Liebman. They have indicated that the religion of the Jewish people cannot be properly understood without its emphasis on seeking moral improvement. The ancient prophets constantly announced to their people what they did *not* want to hear. They dwelled on Israel's alienation from God and failure to live up to His moral requirements. Only after reconciliation with their God and with their fellowman would the Israelites find their inner peace and satisfaction.

Although Judaism is not obsessed with man's sinful nature, the reality of sin and man's life-long need to struggle against his aggressive impulses is a recurring

theme in the Bible and rabbinic theology. Our con-
science serves to remind us that we have gone astray
from our moral direction. Feeling inner peace and con-
tentment when we should feel dissatisfied with poor
moral performance stands in the way of self-improve-
ment. The Book of Deuteronomy describes this mis-
placed peace of mind with the words, "He blesses himself in his heart saying: 'I shall have peace though I walk
in the stubbornness of my heart ...' "

Although religious belief requires a sense of discon-
tent and restlessness, it does not exclude peace of mind
as a secondary goal, a by-product of faith. Such inner
peace may come with the satisfaction of accepting that
which cannot be changed in God's world or with the
feeling that we have made an earnest effort to live a useful and productive life.

What has been said to describe the role of the
prophet can be extended to express the goal of religious
faith: to afflict the comfortable and comfort the afflicted.

GOD
Questioning
Familiar Views

13 Belief in one God is the main contribution of Judaism to civilization

It is commonly believed that the ancient Israelites were alone in their belief in one God, unlike the pagan religions with their emphasis on polytheism—the belief in many gods. However, we may find among some ancient pagan cultures the concept of a single god who is creator, eternal and even all-powerful.

The unique contribution of the Israelites was the belief in a God who is the source of all being and in no way dependent on the world that He created. God does not emerge from any form or power that precedes Him. He is completely free of the limitations of mythology or magic.

Most essential is the idea that the God in whom the ancient Israelites believed was a *moral* God who was not capricious or arbitrary. He made moral demands upon His human creation. Thus it is not monotheism alone that set the Israelites apart but, more precisely, ethical monotheism. It was a qualitative rather than quantitative difference that distinguished the Hebrews from other ancient people.

When the Jew declares his affirmation of faith, "Hear, O Israel, the Lord our God, the Lord is One," he asserts that God is alone and unique, unlike any other being—human or so-called divine.

When the prophets of Israel proclaimed the oneness of God, they went beyond repudiating the worship of idols. They asserted that all mankind was interrelated. Furthermore, they declared that one universal law of righteousness holds sway over all people throughout the world.

Beginning in the sixth century before the Common Era, the numerical oneness of God began to take on importance. Why then? Judaism came into contact with Zoroastrianism with its doctrine of dualism—the belief in two divine powers: the god of light and goodness locked in a struggle with the god of darkness and evil. Religion's purpose, as Zoroastrianism conceived it, is to see that men choose the right divinity.

Judaism rejected the dualism of Zoroastrianism by reaffirming the existence of one God. The prophet of the Exile, Isaiah, insisted that one and the same God fashions light and creates darkness, makes peace and creates evil.

When Christianity became a widely accepted religion, Judaism again asserted the numerical oneness of God in contrast to the Christian dogma of the Trinity. The mother religion repudiated this thesis that God, though one, is at the same time three beings, "Co-eternal and Coequal." In rejecting the Trinity, Judaism reasserted that God was one, an indivisible unity. In the words of Maimonides, "He who brought all things into being and who is their first cause is one."

To sum up, the essential contribution of Judaism was its belief in ethical monotheism. God alone is the source of all goodness: He requires moral standards of all people. The numerical oneness of God assumes importance in Jewish thought only as a reaction to those religions that deny the indivisibility of the one God.

14 God determines the fate of all individuals

It would be simple to accept the thought that an all-knowing God determines the actions of all humans. If that is so, then since God knows everything that happens and will happen to us, His prior knowledge seals our fate. We cannot act as free agents. When Jews use the expression *bashert*, they imply man's inability to counter-act God's knowledge of all future events and His ability to control those events.

But to accept the notion that all occurrences are de-termined in advance by God leaves man without free-dom of thought and action. How does man differ from the animal if he possesses no free will? How can he be regarded as either moral or immoral without the ability to choose the right or wrong path?

The teachers of Judaism were painfully aware of this paradox. They could not surrender the belief in God's omniscience nor could they deny man's freedom of will. The contradiction remains. Rabbi Akiba acknowledged the mystery when he said: "Everything is foreseen, yet free will is given to man."

A later sage, Rabbi Hanina, attempted to go a step farther when he declared: "Everything is in the hands of God except the fear of God." In rabbinic terminology, fear of God (*yirat shamayim*) refers to moral conduct, religion. Rabbi Hanina felt that God determines most of our characteristics—our degree of intelligence, personality, physical features, etc.—but our moral choices are determined exclusively by the individual. Only man can choose the path of good or evil. God, as it were, has relinquished control in the area of man's moral decision-making. "... I have put before you life and death, blessing and curse. Choose life, if you and your offspring would live" (Deut. 30:19).

The medieval Jewish philosophers went to even greater lengths in explaining the importance of free will. Maimonides states: "Any man born is free to become as righteous as Moses, or as wicked as Jeroboam, a student or an ignoramus, kind or cruel, generous or selfish." According to Maimonides, it is God's desire that the individual exercise the power to act according to his own will within the limits of his capacity.

Abraham Ibn David (twelfth cent.), one of the most rationalistic Jewish philosophers, explains the paradox of God's omniscience and man's free will in this way: God in His omniscience knows all the possibilities with which the individual will be confronted, yet God does not know in advance which choice the individual is going to make. This area of human freedom, said Ibn David, is in accordance with God's plan.

We will probably never comprehend the real meaning of God's omniscience since we can define a divine quality only in limited human terms. Nor may we ever fully grasp the extent of man's freedom of will, which choices are within and which beyond His control. Yet Judaism clearly assigns man a major role in which the freedom to choose good and avoid evil is essential. Without free will, religion is reduced to a form of magic.

15   God is totally self-sufficient and does not need man

Since God, unlike man, was not created nor does he have physical needs to sustain Himself, we would assume that God does not really need man. Man exists by virtue of God's grace. Man is in need of God but God is not in need of man.

Yet, this assumption ignores a basic Jewish viewpoint. At the time of creation God entered into a partnership with man. He reacts to man's joys and sorrows and is a participant with man in his struggle to achieve peace and justice in the world.

Since God made man a partner in His enterprise, He needs man to improve upon the world that He deliberately left unfinished, imperfect.

Commenting on the verse in the Psalms, "To God we render strength," the Midrash adds: "When Israel performs the will of God, they add strength to the heavenly power. However, when Israel fails to perform God's will, they weaken, as it were, the great power of Him who is above us." One rabbinic view even depicts God's need to pray. "He recites this prayer: 'May it be My will that My love for humans will overcome my exasperation with them!'"

In Jewish thought, man's relationship to God is never passive. Man is perceived as an active associate with God. "The wicked rely on their gods ... The righteous are a support to God" (Gen. Rabbah, 69:3). Judah Halevi, the medieval Jewish poet, expressed God's need for man in one of his immortal poems: "When I go forth to seek You, I find You seeking me."

The need to be needed is not only a human trait, it is a divine necessity as well. *Hasidic* thought carried the principal of God in need of man even further. The Baal Shem Tov would rebuke his people by quoting the verse, "The Lord is thy shadow" (Ps. 121:5). Just as man's shadow does whatever man does, so does God do, as it were, whatever man does. Just as a man is required to perform good deeds, such as giving charity and showing compassion, so does God follow man's example. God's goodness toward His creatures depends on the way they conduct themselves. Every human act releases a cosmic response: God's favor can flow only from man's behavior. God shows His benevolence when man gives Him the power to do so by practicing benevolence.

This unusually bold view of God as follower expressed by the founder of *Hasidism* would have been rejected outright by most of the medieval Jewish philosophers, who saw God as being independent of His creation, without needs or emotions. To these philosophers a God in need of man implies a less than perfect Being. One of the paradoxes within Judaism is that the independent God of the philosophers is different from the God whom the Jew addresses on a personal level. Yet, Jewish thought accommodates both views—the intellectual concept of a Deity *and* the highly personal view of a God in need of man just as man is in need of Him.

16 Man cannot improve on what a perfect God has created

God's perfection does not preclude man's ability to improve upon what He has created. We are constantly reminded in rabbinic texts that God has created an incomplete world waiting to be improved upon by man. Man has not only the ability but the responsibility to improve upon His creation. Man is regarded as God's partner in the creative process, but with this basic difference: Only God has the unique capacity to create the basic element of life; man can only enhance that which has already been created.

The commandment to circumcise the male child is given as an example of man's ability to improve upon God's creation. By performing the *brit milah* upon the child, man improves upon God's unfinished creation by enabling the child to enter into a higher stage, a covenantal relationship with God.

The physician is likewise regarded as an agent of God sent to improve upon God's handiwork. A surgeon is not only permitted but morally required to use his skill to restore the health of a patient born with a congenital defect. The physician who would refuse to operate on his patient because he felt that he must not interfere with an "act of God" or with "God's will" fails to grasp his religious responsibility to his profession, to God and man. To improve upon that which God has created is not an act of heresy; it is a religious requirement for those who are blessed with special skills.

The question of elective cosmetic surgery has been discussed by Jewish legal authorities. The problem in Jewish law associated with plastic surgery is whether or not such procedures violate the clear prohibition against wounding the body which must be done in order to improve the patient's appearance. There is also the risk to life when general anesthesia is administered. Some authorities question whether elective cosmetic surgery is permissible for the sole purpose of beautification. Surgery is generally permitted to alleviate physical pain and even emotional anguish, but whether elective cosmetic surgery qualifies under these conditions may be widely interpreted.

The interpretation of the Five Books of Moses carried with it the problem of whether the original God-given text may be expanded and clarified through human interpretation. The ancient Sadducees, the priestly aristocratic class known for their conservatism, were against rabbinic interpretations since they did not come from Mt. Sinai as the original text of the Torah. The Pharisees, the scholarly class formed from the Jewish laity, felt that both the Bible and its interpretations by the rabbis were sanctioned by God and that both came from Mt. Sinai. What is the difference between the biblical text and the later rabbinic interpretation? *Seder Eliyahu Zuta* offers a parable to explain.

A human king had two servants whom he loved dearly. To each of them he gave a *kab* of wheat (about two quarts) and a bundle of flax. What did the wiser of them do? He took the flax and wove a cloth from it, and from the wheat he made flour which he sifted and milled and made bread which he arranged on the table, covering it with the cloth. He left it for the king's arrival. The foolish one did nothing.

Later the king returned home and said: "My sons, bring me what I gave to you." One brought the fine bread on the table, covered with a cloth; the other brought the wheat in a box with the bundle of flax on top. What shame! What embarrassment! Which then is dearer to the king? The one who brought out the table with the fine bread on it. Thus, when God gave the Torah to Israel He gave it to them as wheat from which to produce the fine flour and as flax from which to produce cloth.

Simcha Bunam of Przysucha comments on God's unfinished world: "The Lord created the world in a state of beginning. The universe is always in an incomplete state, in the form of its beginning. It is not like a vessel at which the master works to finish it; it requires continuous labor by creative forces. Should these cease for only a second, the universe would return to its primeval chaos."

ETHICS
More Than
Meets the Eye

17 Anyone who observes the commandments is defined as a religious Jew

Jews who scrupulously follow the law in their personal lives are generally called religious. It is for this reason that many Jews who do not observe the religious commandments voluntarily exclude themselves from the "religious" community with their response, "You know, I'm not at all religious!" In contemporary Hebrew as well, an observant Jew is usually referred to as *dati*, which connotes a religious person.

The accepted word for religion, *dat*, was not used in the Talmudic period. *Yirat shamayim* — literally, fear of Heaven — comes closest to the classical definition of religion. Yet this fear of Heaven does not imply that a tyrannical God is anxious to punish wrongdoers for the slightest infraction of His laws. *Yirat shamayim* refers to a feeling of awe before God whose ways man cannot begin to fathom but for whom he has supreme regard and reverence.

A religious Jew then is one who out of reverence for God chooses to observe the ritual along *with* the moral laws prescribed in the Torah. He is not regarded as religious if he chooses to follow only those ritual *mitzvot* between man and God and avoids the ethical laws that are called *mitzvot* between man and man. The laws regarding business ethics, treatment of the aged, and behavior toward the stranger are no less binding than the dietary laws or observance of the Sabbath and festivals. To call the person who observes only the ritual laws and neglects the ethical laws a religious Jew runs contrary to the word and spirit of the prophets and the rabbinical authorities.

Likewise, anyone who observes the commandments merely out of custom or habit cannot be deemed religious. He may be seen as observant, but to be called religious would be inappropriate because he does not make a conscious decision to improve his character through his observance of the *mitzvot*. "The *mitzvot* were given expressly to purify mankind" (Gen. Rabbah 44:1).

It is unfortunate that in the public mind only those who observe the ceremonial laws of Judiasm are called *dati-im*, religious persons. Several years ago Rabbi Louis I. Rabinowitz addressed this problem in an article appearing in *Conservative Judaism*.

Rabinowitz indicated that there were apartment houses and developments erected by *dati-im*, and only those who adhered to the requirements of *dat* were permitted to live in them. A resident who was discovered riding or smoking on the Sabbath would automatically lose his right to his home; by his conduct he was no longer a *dati*. If, however, such a resident were to be found guilty of a crime in the area of commercial law or sexual offenses, he would not forfeit his right to be considered *dati* as long as he publicly continued to adhere to the criteria of religiosity. His action might be deplored, he would be regarded as not having done "the right thing," but his status as *dati* would not necessarily be deleteriously affected.

The question has repeatedly been asked whether a person who does not observe the rituals yet who stands in awe before the mystery of God's creation can be called religious. Albert Einstein did not hesitate to characterize himself as a religious man:

> To know that what is impenetrable to us really exists, manifesting itself as the highest wisdom and most radiant beauty which our dull faculties can comprehend only in their primitive forms — this knowledge, this feeling is the center of true religiousness. In this sense and in this sense only, I belong to the ranks of devoutly religious men (*The New York Times*, April 19, 1955).

Anatoly Shcharansky expressed a similar mystical feeling when he addressed an American audience for the first time in 1986 after his release from Russian imprisonment: "All the resources of a superpower cannot isolate a man who hears the voice of freedom, a voice I heard from the very chamber of my soul."

In light of the testimony of these rare individuals and others who have lived intensely moral lives under adverse conditions, it would be appropriate to refer to such people as religious even though their religiosity differs from the conventional definition.

18 Jewish law favors capital punishment

There is no question that the Torah refers to capital punishment for various crimes. The three methods of executing criminals were by stoning, burning and hanging. The Talmud refers to four methods of execution: stoning, burning, slaying (by the sword) and strangling. Nevertheless, to conclude that Jewish law advocates capital punishment is a misrepresentation. There is sufficient evidence in the Talmud that the death penalty was rarely applied after the destruction of Jerusalem in the year 70 C.E.

To begin with, it was not easy to convict someone of a crime that was punishable by death. In the rabbinic courts circumstantial evidence was not admitted. The law required at least two witnesses to the crime, a requisite that prevented most cases from coming to trial. The witnesses were questioned separately regarding the exact place and time of the crime and their recognition of the accused. If there was any discrepancy in their testimony, the accused was immediately acquitted. Furthermore, the witnesses had had to warn the accused that he was about to commit a crime that carried the death penalty. The accused had to reject the warning and proceed to commit the criminal act fully conscious of the nature and consequences of his crime.

Once the case came before the judges, a majority of one was sufficient to acquit the accused; a plurality of two was required to convict. Furthermore, there had to be at least one judge in the court who argued in favor of acquittal. If the decision to convict was unanimous, collusion was suspected. Unlike the case with noncapital crimes, a judge who voted for acquittal could not then change his vote for conviction, yet he was free to change his vote in favor of acquittal. A verdict to acquit could be handed down on the same day of the trial, but not a verdict of conviction.

The judges sat in a semi-circle, with the younger members of the court on the sides and the elders toward the middle. When the vote was called, the younger judges rendered their decision prior to their elders so that they might not be unduly influenced by the verdict of the more experienced judges.

Once the sentence was pronounced, every consideration was given to permit a reversal of the verdict before the actual execution. New evidence was accepted until the last moment before the execution.

If the accused claimed that he had some new argument in favor of his acquittal, he had to be brought back from the field to the courtroom as many as four or five times "provided there was something of substance in his words."

George Foot Moore, commenting on all the laws on behalf of the accused, concluded: "It is clear that with such a procedure conviction in capital cases was next to impossible, and that this was the intention of the framers of the rules is equally plain."

Decades after the Romans removed from the Sanhedrin the right of imposing capital punishment, several prominent scholars engaged in an academic discussion on capital punishment. Their views, found in the Mishna Makkot, express their revulsion against capital punishment even though it had been sanctioned in the past.

A Sanhedrin that puts a man to death once in seven years is called destructive. Rabbi Eleazar Ben Azariah says, "Or once in seventy years." Rabbi Tarfon and Rabbi Akiba said, "If we had been in the Sanhedrin no death sentence would ever have been passed." Rabbi Simeon ben Gamliel said: "If so, they would have multiplied murderers in Israel"(1:10).

The Talmud asks whether Rabbi Eleazar's statement was a criticism of the old Sanhedrin or whether it described how rare death sentences were. The question is left without a decisive answer. Rabbi Tarfon and Rabbi Akiba probably meant that they would have examined the witnesses so intensely that they would have confused them or made them contradict themselves.

19   Ancient Judaism approved
of the institution of slavery

The Hebrew Bible did not seek the abolishment of slavery nor did it condemn the institution of slavery, but nowhere do we find that the ownership of slaves was condoned or encouraged in the biblical text. When we compare the biblical attitude toward slavery with the views of Plato and Aristotle, who influenced their Greek contemporaries hundreds of years after the biblical age, we detect dramatic differences beween the two cultures.

Plato encouraged contempt for slaves as a lower class of humans. Even if a master killed his own slave, all he needed to do was undergo a form of purification. Aristotle regarded slavery as natural and normal. "For that some should rule, and others be ruled is a thing, not only necessary, but expedient; from the hour of their birth, some are marked out for subjection, others for rule." By contrast, neither the Bible nor the Talmud makes any attempt to defend the need to hold slaves.

Slavery existed in ancient Israel just as it was prevalent among all civilizations with whom the Israelites came into contact. Yet, the Torah is sensitive to the treatment of slaves. Time and again the Israelites were reminded that they were once slaves in the land of Egypt. Hebrew slaves enjoyed more rights than heathen slaves, and neither kind could be treated harshly by their masters.

An Israelite could become a slave only if he defaulted on his debt or if he could not pay the penalty for stealing. He could also submit himself into slavery because of poverty. He was to serve his master for six years only; on the seventh year he was required to be set free. By limiting the years of enslavement, the Bible indicated that it was not in favor of slavery but recognized it as a prevalent evil. Moreover, the slave's master was responsible for securing the slave's future so that he would not return to slavery. "You shall not let him go empty, you shall furnish him liberally out of your flock, and out of your threshing floor, and out of your winepress ..." (Deut. 15:13-14).

As members of his master's household, a Hebrew slave was entitled to enjoy Sabbath rest and partake of the Passover sacrifical meal. He was permitted to own and acquire property. His master could not abuse him physically or impose a physical burden upon him that he could not endure. A runaway slave was required to be given refuge and not to be returned to his master. A slave who was physically impaired by his master was automatically released. The killing of a slave was as serious a crime as the killing of a free man, whether the perpetrator was his master or someone else. There were so many restrictions placed upon the master that the rabbis later commented on their relationship: "He who buys a Hebrew slave buys a master."

The heathen slave did not enjoy the same privileges as the Israelite slave—he became his master's property—but Jewish law was also sensitive to his needs. He too was set free if he suffered physical injury by the hand of his owner. Likewise, the master who killed a heathen slave was subject to the death penalty. The non-Jewish slave also was entitled to rest on the Sabbath with the other members of his master's household.

It is important to observe how the medieval scholar Moses Maimonides dealt with the institution of slavery as found in the Bible and the Talmud. He was not free to abrogate biblical law, yet he sought to mitigate the sacred law by placing even greater responsibilities upon the master.

> It is permissible to make a Canaanite slave work with rigor; but while this is the law, the ways of ethics and prudence require that the master should be just and merciful, not to make the burden too heavy on his slave and not press him too hard; he should give him of all food and drink ... Slaves may not be mistreated or offended. The law destined them for service, not for humiliation. Do not shout at them or be angry with them, but listen to their complaints. (*Yad*, *"Avadim"* 9:8).

In his *Guide for the Perplexed* (3:39), Maimonides reminds the master of a slave : "He ought to rise and advance with you, be with you in the place you choose for yourself, and when fortune is good to you, do not grudge him his portion."

20 Judaism teaches that people are inherently moral

The claim that Judaism believes in the basic goodness of man is really an oversimplification of a complex theme in Jewish thought.

Observers have often attempted to show that, unlike Christianity with its concept of Original Sin whereby all descendants of Adam have inherited sinfulness from the first man, Judaism regards man as innately moral. But the Torah and the Talmud recognize man in a more realistic light. He is inherently prone to both virtue *and* sin. True, man is created in God's image and is therefore endowed with the *capacity* to choose good over evil, yet the desire and effort to overcome the evil impulse is often lacking. The struggle to conquer aggressiveness and destructiveness must begin early in life, yet we are never free of that inner conflict until the day of death.

In spite of the never-ending struggle with the evil impulse, Judaism does not regard man as being trapped by evil forces beyond his control. He is not a helpless victim of fate. Nor does his soul need to be "saved" by God; it is in no way imprisoned by the body.

There is no term in Hebrew to express salvation through God's grace in which a man is rescued from his human unworthiness.

The presence of the aggressive impulse is not always looked upon as harmful or destructive. Otherwise, why would a beneficent God have implanted the aggressive drive within man in the first place?

The Sages comment on the verse in Genesis: "And God saw everything that He had made, and behold, it was very good." "Very good," they explained, refers to the two drives, the *yetzer hatov* and *yetzer hara*, the spiritual impulse and the aggressive impulse. "But how can the aggressive impulse be called 'very good?'" they asked. And their response: "Were it not for that drive, a man would not build a house, marry a wife, beget children or engage in business affairs" (Gen. Rabbah 9:7). How man chooses to handle his aggressive drives is most crucial.

Whatever struggles the individual has to cope with to prevent the domination of the *yetzer hara*, Judaism holds tenaciously to the belief in mankind's continuous progress toward the ideal state culminating in the Messianic Era. In spite of occasional reversals, mankind continues to move inexorably forward to higher stages of development when evil will give way to the triumph of righteousness.

21 All forms of gambling are regarded as sinful

The fact that so many laws and enactments dealing with gambling have been written indicates the seriousness of the problem in Jewish communities over many centuries.

As far back as Mishnaic times (first and second centuries) two types of professional gamblers were prohibited from giving testimony in a Jewish court of law: those who threw dice and those who bet on pigeon races (Sanhedrin 3:3).

The reasons that the rabbis frowned upon those occupied in gambling were varied. Gamblers were seen as moral weaklings who couldn't withstand temptation; they were distracted from the study of Torah and from a gainful occupation; they took funds that did not rightfully belong to them; they neglected the opportunity to improve society.

Some rabbis objected even to occasional gambling. Others were more flexible: They permitted gambling on festive occasions such as Hanukkah and Purim and at special family gatherings and occasions when sociability was encouraged.

Many rabbinic responsa during the Middle Ages deal with the moral issue of gambling. Some rabbis differentiated between gambling for private gain and giving away one's winnings for charitable purposes. Generally, the authorities approved of games of chance where all or part of the winnings were given over to charity.

The *Code of Jewish Law*, which presented the final decision on legal questions, was cognizant of the wide practice of occasional gambling and permitted it.

One receives the impression that the Jewish authorities would have preferred to prohibit gambling altogether, yet they were pressured into accepting it as an occasional or mild form of recreation. When the masses and even some prominent rabbis indulged in the gambling spirit, the law made some accommodation by requiring moderation rather than its abolition. Thus, respect for the law could be ensured and the gambling habit could be kept under control.

22 Lying is wrong
under all circumstances

Truth, *emet*, is one of the essential principles of Judaism. The Bible frequently describes God as "The God of Truth." The Talmud as well speaks of truth as the "Seal of God." Since God never deviates from the truth, only the person who consistently speaks the truth can aspire to the religious goal of imitating God.

From various Talmudic sources we see the value that the rabbis place upon telling the truth. "Let your yea and nay be both righteous; do not speak with your mouth what you do not mean in your heart." Rabbi Simeon says: "The punishment of the liar is that he is not believed even when he speaks the truth." Rabbi Ze'era says :"One must not promise to give something to a child, and not give it to him; in so doing he is taught to lie."

Yet, there are rare occasions when compromising the truth is condoned, especially in order to preserve peace.

Great is peace since for the sake of peace the Holy One altered a statement. When God reported Sarah's statement to Abraham, He quotes her as saying,"Indeed, shall I who am old bear a child?" (Gen. 18:13), when in fact, she had said, "My lord [Abraham] being old." Thus, to preserve peace in the household, God omitted Sarah's slight to her husband (Yebamot 65b).

So great is peace, says Rabbi Simeon Ben Lakish, that the Torah alters the truth to create peace between Joseph and his brothers. The brothers sent this message to Joseph: "Your father left this instruction before his death, saying, 'Forgive, I urge you, the offense and guilt of your brothers.'" But we do not find in the Torah that Jacob had given any such command. *The Scripture used fictitious words for the sake of peace.*

Aaron the High Priest would also tell a white lie in order to promote peace between neighbors. When two men had quarreled, Aaron went and sat near one and said "See what your neighbor says: He is rending his heart and tearing his garments, and saying, 'Woe is me, how shall I lift up my eyes and look on my neighbor? I am ashamed because of him, for I have sinned against him.'" And he sat with him until he had removed hatred from the man's heart. Then he went and spoke the same words to the other man. When these two men met, they embraced and kissed each other.

Here then we have several examples indicating that the truth may be bent in order to bring about domestic peace. As important as truth-telling is, the virtue of establishing peace takes priority.

In the Talmud Rabbi Judah says in the name of Samuel: Learned men may conceal the truth regarding the following three matters: *tractate*, *sex* and *hospitality*.

Tractate: A scholar may declare that he is unfamiliar with a section of the Mishna in order not to flaunt his intellectual ability.

Sex: A scholar need not give a candid response if he is asked embarrassing questions about his marital life.

Hospitality: A scholar who has been warmly received

by his host may refrain from reporting the truth about his reception if he feels that the host will be barraged by unwelcome guests.

Truth implies trust and confidence. We must be able to *assume* that other people are telling us the truth; otherwise no trusting relationship can ever endure among family members, friends or business associates. However, compromising the truth in order to achieve an even higher good can be justified in exceptional circumstances. Judaism differs with the position of Immanuel Kant, who claimed that one must not deviate from the truth even if it means revealing the whereabouts of his friend which would cause his certain death. Even telling the truth has its limitations, especially when it results in tragic consequences.

SEX AND BIRTH
Lesser Known Views

23 The offspring of an unmarried couple is regarded as illegitimate

Jewish law maintains that sexual intimacy is proper only within marriage. Jews, however, do not refer to a single man and woman who are intimate as "living in sin," a concept familiar to Christians.

Jewish law does not regard a sexual relationship between an unmarried couple with the same severity as it does an adulterous relationship between married people, nor is a child born to an unmarried couple considered a *mamzer* (bastard). This term is restricted to offspring of an unlawful, incestuous or adulterous marriage.

The problem of intimacy among engaged couples is not confined to the contemporary scene. According to the Jewish codes, sexual relations between an engaged couple is not prohibited biblically, only rabbinically. In the Mishnaic period — the first two centuries of the Common Era — intimacy among engaged couples was permitted among Jews living in Judea, but not in the Galilee area. Eventually the stricter Galilean rule was adopted for all engaged couples.

To discourage intimacy among engaged couples a change had to be made in the marriage ritual. At one time two separate ceremonies took place at least several months apart — betrothal and then marriage. Even as late as the Middle Ages these two ceremonies were not celebrated together. However, the rabbinical authorities were concerned with the problem of sexual intimacy between the time of the betrothal ceremony and the marriage; they decided to combine the two ceremonies, and this procedure eventually became acceptable at all Jewish weddings.

To sum up, most rabbinical authorities opposed all sexual relationships before marriage whether the couple contemplated marriage or not. Even though a clear-cut reason for prohibiting premarital sex was absent from the Bible, sons and daughters were expected to observe the fifth commandment, honoring the moral code of one's parents. A child born out of wedlock, however, is in no way stigmatized in the same way as the offspring of an adulterous relationship.

24 Judaism advocates sex for procreation, not for pleasure

Although procreation is an essential goal of marriage, the pleasure of sexual activity between husband and wife is also advocated in Jewish law. For example, those who are aged, infirm or sterile are nevertheless encouraged to marry even when procreation is not possible.

Jewish sources are explicit in requiring husband and wife to derive pleasure in their sexual intimacy which has been ordained by God and is therefore a sacred act. The Talmud advises scholars and their wives to engage in sexual activity on Sabbath Eve because the Sabbath is reserved for pleasure, rest and physical enjoyment

Moses Maimonides expresses a minority view when he asserts: "The purpose of intercourse is to perpetuate the species, not for the pleasure of the act alone." It has been suggested that Maimonides was unduly influenced by Greek thought in separating the spiritual from the physical pleasures. Nahmanides, another great authority and admirer of Maimonides, challenges his mentor for his reliance on Aristotle, especially when the Greek philosopher taught that the sense of touch was the lowliest of the five senses. Nahmanides says:

> But we who have the Torah and believe that God created everything in His wisdom do not believe that He created anything inherently ugly or unseemly. If

we were to say that intercourse is repulsive then we blaspheme God who created the genitals.

Nahmanides concludes that "sexual intercourse is holy and pure when conducted properly, in the appropriate time and with the proper intentions."

Another prominent authority, Rabbi Jacob Emden (eighteenth cent.), comments:

The wise men of other nations claim that the sense of touch is a disgrace. To us the sexual act is worthy, good and beneficial even to the soul. No other human activity compares with it. When performed with pure and clean intention it is certainly holy.

One reason that some people are under the mistaken impression that Judaism advocates sex only for procreation is their confusion with the classical Christian attitude toward sex. Paul, who was influenced by Greek culture, believed that the body and soul were in perpetual conflict. The soul was perfect and sinless, the body corrupt and sinful. Therefore, man must suppress the physical and strive to live exclusively on the spiritual level. Paul, himself a celibate, wished others to follow his example. However, since most people could not attain the ideal of celibacy, marriage was permitted as a concession to human weakness. According to Paul, marriage could be justified by God only for the purpose of procreation and not enjoyment. Paul's views on sex and marriage were accepted by believing Christians for centuries and to this day is accepted by some Catholics. Hence, marriage continues to be forbidden to members of the Catholic clergy.

In stark contrast to this view, classical Judaism regarded marriage and sexual intimacy as a sacred act whether for the purpose of procreation or not. Only a small minority did not accept this view.

25 Jewish law is totally opposed to birth control

Although the great majority of Jewish couples practice some form of birth control, many of these couples assume that they are contravening Jewish law. Since the first commandment that appears in the Torah is to "be fruitful and multiply," Jewish law does not tolerate any exception to this biblical injunction.

This widely held assumption requires clarification. The duty to give birth to children is a religious requirement. A couple that voluntarily decides not to raise a family for personal or economic reasons chooses to ignore a basic Jewish principle.

Furthermore, the following biblical passage in Genesis 38 has been cited as the course prohibiting birth control:

> But Onan, knowing that the seed would not count as his, *let it go to waste* whenever he joined with his brother's wife, so as not to provide offspring for his brother. What he did was displeasing to the Lord, and He took his life also.

The rabbis derive from this passage that "to let one's seed go to waste" is sinful.

However, the rabbinic authorities declared exceptions to the rule where there were extenuating circumstances. A woman may sterilize herself if the pain of childbearing is intolerable. The rabbis also permitted a woman to avoid pregnancy if she previously gave birth to degenerate offspring and feared giving birth to other problem children.

The classical source on the subject of birth control is the debate between Rabbi Meir and the Sages (second cent. C.E.). Rabbi Meir declared that "Three women use a *mokh* (absorbent) during intercourse." These are a minor, a pregnant woman and a nursing mother. Meir's reasoning was that in each case pregnancy could injure the health of the mother. The minor would not be strong enough to endure the rigors of pregnancy for nine months; the fetus carried by a pregnant woman could die if she conceived again; a nursing mother who became pregnant would cease to produce milk, thus endangering the life of her infant. The Sages differ with Rabbi Meir regarding the minor. They would prefer to rely on God's compassion to protect her.

This passage presents problems in light of our present knowledge. We know, for example, that a woman does not become pregnant again while carrying a fetus. Further, we do not know exactly the function or the effectiveness of the absorbent. Most puzzling, however, we are not certain from the text whether Rabbi Meir *requires* that the absorbent be used or whether he *permits* its use in these three cases.

Later authorities debated the question of whether these three categories of women may practice birth control, while others may not, or whether these are required to practice birth control while others are permitted should a health problem arise. Most traditional authorities interpret the text to permit contraceptive devices when it has been clearly established that a pregnancy would be injurious to the mother.

26 Judaism makes no allowance for terminating pregnancy

Unlike Catholicism, Judaism does not regard abortion as a form of murder. However, abortion is prohibited if the mother merely does not wish to give birth to a child. Only when the life or health of the mother is threatened do most rabbis permit therapeutic abortion.

Some rabbinic authorities are more stringent than others, permitting abortion only when the mother's life is in danger or where her health may be adversely affected if her pregnancy is allowed to continue. Others are more lenient: they sanction therapeutic abortion where there was incest or rape, or even fear that the infant may be malformed. They reason that priority must be given to the concerns of the mother and that giving birth under such traumatic circumstances would harm her emotional health, causing her to suffer shame or anguish. This more lenient view is not acceptable to many Orthodox rabbinical authorities but is generally accepted by Conservative and Reform rabbis.

Rabbi Isaac Klein, who was a leading authority in the Conservative rabbinate, presented the following guidelines regarding abortion:

In the later stages (of pregnancy) we would permit abortion only when the birth of the fetus would be a direct threat to the life of the mother. This threat should be interpreted to include cases where continuation of the pregnancy would have such a debilitating effect, psychological or otherwise, on the mother as to constitute a hazard to her life, however remote such danger may be.

In the earlier stages we would allow therapeutic abortions whenever there is a threat to the health of the mother, directly or indirectly, physically or psychologically. Since such an interpretation is very flexible and therefore subject to abuse, the facts have to be established by reliable medical evidence (*Conservative Judaism*, Vol. 24, No. 3, 1970).

27   A child must be named
after a deceased relative

Contrary to popular opinion, there are no legal requirements regarding the naming of a child, only that the child be given a Hebrew name.

For example, Sephardic Jews (those originating from Middle Eastern countries) name a child after a living person. A son is frequently named after his living grandfather. Ashkenazim (originally from Central and Eastern Europe) usually follow the custom of naming a child after a deceased relative.

We are not certain as to why the two communities follow different practices. One theory is that Ashkenazic Jews associated the name with the person's soul. Therefore, to name a child after a living person could shorten the years of that person. Although the religious authorities were probably aware that this belief was based on superstition, they discouraged the custom of naming the child after a living person for a more practical reason: to have two people in one family with the same name would lead to confusion.

Ashkenazic children have not always been named after a deceased relative. Some children bear the name of eminent Jewish personalities. Among the *hasidim* it was the custom to name the children after the rabbi who most influenced the family.

Since there are no specific laws regarding the giving of names, some children are named in connection with significant events. This tradition dates back to biblical times when events in the family or community inspired the naming of a newborn. In Israel today this tradition has been restored. Hence, the names of many Israelis are based on celebrated events relating to the State of Israel.

Some parents choose a Hebrew name because they are impressed with its meaning. Or a child will be given a pleasant sounding name which merely appeals to the parents. No one need question the propriety of these Hebrew names.

28   A male child is not a Jew until he is circumcised

The ceremony of circumcision does not "make" a child Jewish. If his mother is Jewish, he becomes a Jew at birth. The moment the child is born he is automatically a descendant of Abraham, the first Hebrew. The commandment of circumcision (*brit milah*) reinforces that identification with his people. By bearing a sign sealed in his flesh, he formally enters a covenant which binds him to all the children of Israel. Although the son is regarded as Jew by birth, his father has not fulfilled his responsibility to God, to his child and to the Jewish people unless he accepts the obligation of seeing that his son is circumcised according to Jewish law.

If the child were not considered Jewish until the time of circumcision — the eighth day — he would be in a state of limbo without any religious identity. Furthermore, if the infant is ill and the physician advises a postponement of the *brit milah*, the surgery must be delayed for as long as the doctor deems necessary. In that case, the *brit milah* is performed seven days after the infant's recovery from a general disease or immediately after recovery from a minor illness, such as a slight eye disorder.

The Jewish sources also refer to a situation where "two brothers have died as a result of circumcision." This probably refers to a case of hemophilia in the family. Circumcision is not permitted under these circumstances until it is certain that the child will not be affected. It is also possible that the child may have to forgo circumcision altogether where his life would be endangered. In spite of this seeming disability, the child is regarded as a Jew without qualification.

In contradistinction to a child born to a Jewish mother, a candidate for conversion cannot be considered Jewish until he is circumcised according to Jewish law.

Although an uncircumcised infant is regarded as a Jew from birth, the question arises whether he may become a *bar mitzvah* without *brit milah*. Unless there are extenuating circumstances, such as hemophilia, traditional authorities would not permit the child to be called to the Torah unless he has been circumcised.

WOMEN'S ROLE
Varied Opinions, Surprising Responses

29 A woman may not come in physical contact with a Torah Scroll

Many Jews who themselves do not personally accept the Orthodox law stating that a menstruating woman is in a state of ritual uncleanliness nevertheless disapprove of a woman touching or holding a Torah lest she transmit her "impurity" to a sacred object.

It is this objection to transmitting "impurity" that prompts some Jews to oppose calling women for an *aliyah* to the Torah. However, the legal authorities did not object to a woman coming into physical contact with the Torah Scroll even if she were a menstruant. The reason that the more traditional synagogues do not call women to the Torah is based on an entirely different rationale. At one time it was customary for each person called to the Torah to read his portion of the Torah in addition to reciting the blessings. Now if a woman was learned and could read her portion, she would embarrass those male members of the congregation who were unable to read their Torah portion. To prevent feelings of humiliation among the men, the authorities decided that it was prudent not to call women to the Torah.

The Talmud contains a discussion on this very question (Berakhot 22a). Rabbi Judah Ben Bathyra used to say, "Words of the Torah are not susceptible to uncleanness." A student of Rabbi Judah was called upon to read from the Torah and he proceeded to mumble the words in the presence of his teacher. He did not consider it proper to pronounce the words of the Holy Torah clearly since he was in a state of ritual impurity. His teacher directed him to open his mouth and recite the words clearly "for words of the Torah are not susceptible to uncleanness."

The reason the Torah is beyond defilement is not expressly stated. Apparently the Torah, being the most sacred object of the Jewish people, possesses such a high degree of holiness that it is unaffected by the person who comes into contact with it.

30 In Jewish law a woman cannot initiate divorce

The opinion held by many people that only the husband can initiate a Jewish divorce stems from the divorce procedure followed by traditional Jews. On the basis of the Book of Deuteronomy only the husband divorces his wife, and Jewish law still requires the husband to give his wife a "Bill of Divorcement," commonly known as a *get*. It would appear then that the husband is in control of matters of divorce and that any decision to initiate the separation rests solely with him. However, Jewish law does provide the wife with grounds for divorce, and when the Jewish courts were autonomous they had the power to compel the husband to grant his wife a divorce.

It is not generally known that an enactment (*takkanah*) handed down by Rabbi Gershom of Maintz (c. 1000) protected the woman so that she no longer had to consent to a divorce against her will. This enactment was accepted by all Ashkenazic Jews and eventually by Sephardic Jewry in accordance with contemporary Israeli law.

Under what circumstances may a woman demand a divorce? *When the man has certain physical defects* or *if his conduct toward her is offensive*.

Regarding physical defects, the wife is entitled to ask for a divorce if she can prove that he is incapable of producing children or if he has a skin disease that inhibits her enjoyment of sex. However, if the wife married her husband with the knowledge of these defects or if she continued to live with him after learning about them, she does not have legitimate grounds for divorce.

Moses Maimonides expands on the woman's right to seek a divorce:

> If she claims that he is repulsive to me and I cannot bear having intercourse with him, he is forced to divorce her, for she is not his captive and does not have to live with one hateful to her (*Mishneh Torah*, *"Hilkhot Ishut"* 14:8).

Regarding offensive conduct toward one's wife, Jewish law grants the woman much latitude. The wife may ask for a divorce if her husband refuses to maintain her when he has difficulty earning a livelihood. Also she has grounds for divorce if her husband habitually assaults or insults her or if he constantly quarrels in the home, leaving her little choice but to seek an end to the marriage. Similarly, the woman may demand a divorce if her husband "transgresses the Mosaic Law," for example, if he causes her to transgress the dietary laws knowing that she wishes to observe them. Generally, unworthy conduct toward one's wife that makes living together painful is sufficient reason for her to initiate a divorce. In the words of the Talmud: "A wife is given in order that she should live and not to suffer pain."

Although some of the most prominent legal authorities were intent on protecting the woman's rights within marriage, in practice the husband continued to receive favored treatment based on the Talmudic principle that he creates the bond of marriage and he alone may sever it, regardless of his personality or character traits.

Even in the modern era the woman seeking a divorce has had to rely on the consent of her husband. The rabbinic courts could show compassion for her desperate situation, but with the separation of Church and State these courts no longer possessed the judicial power to coerce the husband to accept their decision. A vindictive husband knew that he could not be punished for refusal to grant his wife a religious divorce.

The problem persists to the present day, and since Jewish law requires a *get* in order to remarry, many religiously oriented women remain *agunot* (anchored wives, sing.: *agunah*), dependent on the whim of a recalcitrant husband. The Conservative rabbinate has responded to this injustice by applying an old annulment procedure to mitigate the status of the woman seeking termination of the marriage. The Orthodox rabbinate is also grappling with the problem in response to the pleas of a growing number of women within their movement. However, the major obstacle — relying on the husband's consent to the divorce — has not been overcome. The Reform movement recognizes the civil divorce as binding and does not require the issuing of a *get* before remarriage.

31 Only a woman may kindle the Sabbath candles

The primary responsibility for lighting the Sabbath candles belongs to women. Two reasons are given in Jewish tradition for entrusting her with the obligation. Rashi comments that since Eve committed the first transgression in the Garden of Eden, thus causing the light of the world to be dimmed, the Jewish woman is required as expiation to kindle the Sabbath candles and restore the brightness of that light.

The second reason is more generous and realistic. The Jewish woman is largely responsible for bringing peace, serenity and warmth into the home. Thus, she is given the privilege of initiating the Sabbath by kindling the lights.

Contrary to popular belief, the responsibility of lighting the Sabbath candles does not belong exclusively to women, however. When the woman of the household is absent or incapable of performing the *mitzvah* – if she is ill or giving birth, for example, or if a man lives alone – the man is obligated to light the Sabbath candles.

The general rule is that lighting the Sabbath candles is a religious requirement signaling the beginning of the Sabbath; both men and women are obligated to see that the *mitzvah* is fulfilled.

32   Women had no influence outside the home in biblical times

There is no question that the woman living in biblical times did not enjoy the same status as the man. For example, if she made a vow, her father could annul it before her marriage; after her marriage, her husband was empowered to annul it (Num. 30:2-17). If a girl was violated and the court established her innocence, her father received compensation for the injury (Deut. 22:29).

In spite of their inferior status, women in the biblical era did not live secluded lives. Many activities outside the home were shared by men and women together. In the earlier biblical period, they tended the flock together with the male shepherds and gathered with them at the watering trough — a popular meeting place for young people.

When the sanctuary was being built, women shared the work with the men, and they joined them there for worship and observance of the Holy Days. Occasionally, they were included in the political organization of the nation or tribe and were present at councils with the male leadership. At public celebrations and at weddings, women could be seen and heard as dancers and singers. They sat with the men at public meals. At funerals, they led the procession and chanted dirges which they composed. On rare occasions, they even participated in warfare along with the male population.

Women were also visible in the business world. Chapter 31 of the Book of Proverbs describes the "woman of valor" who engages in commerce, even in the purchase of land.

When the great religious assemblies were convened, the women were participants. When Israel entered into the covenant with God in the time of Moses, the women were included. Women also gathered with the men at Mt. Ebal when Joshua read the Torah in the presence of the Israelites. The requirement to conduct a public reading of the Torah every seven years on the holiday of Sukkot included the participation of women.

In sum, during the biblical era, women did not enjoy the legal rights extended to men, yet, socially they were visible in almost every area of public life. In fact, they enjoyed greater mobility in the biblical than in the Talmudic period. Some modern scholars surmise that the extensive Hellenic influence on Jewish life in the Talmudic period was responsible for this radical change from social mobility to a more secluded life within the home. We have ample documentation indicating the limited role of women in Athenian society. Their essential function was to bear children, to manage the household, and to accept confinement without objection.

33   It is improper for a woman to wear a *tallit*

If Jewish law were decided by public opinion, a woman would be restricted from wearing a *tallit* (prayer shawl) in the synagogue. The few women who choose to pray in a *tallit* continue to attract stares for accepting a religious obligation not required of them.

Those acquainted with the law, however, are aware that the outstanding legal authorities did not protest against women wishing to assume this added obligation. There is only one source found in the Jerusalem Talmud which regards the prayer shawl as a male garment which may not be worn by a woman (according to the law found in Deut. 22:5).   Another source cautions that when a woman puts on a *tallit* she may wish to flaunt her religious piety (*yohara*), an attitude which should be discouraged.

In spite of these two objections, the weight of scholarly opinion is on the side of permitting a woman to wrap herself in a *tallit* during prayer. The issue that divides the rabbinic scholars is centered around this question: May a woman, who, admittedly, is not required to wear a *tallit*, recite the blessing, "Praised are You ... who has commanded us to wear the fringes?"

Rabbenu Tam (d. 1171), a leading French scholar, observes that the Talmudic sage, Rabbi Joseph, though blind, rejoiced in performing commandments from which he was legally exempted. Rabbenu Tam concluded that, in the same manner, women who elect to perform *mitzvot* from which they are exempt, may recite the blessing upon performing the commandment. The opposing view is expressed by Maimonides who rules that, while a woman may choose to wear a *tallit* or fulfill other commandments from which she is exempt, she may not recite the accompanying blessing which concludes with the words, "who has *commanded us* to ...." The *Code of Jewish Law* supports the view of Maimonides, while the great legal authority, Rabbi Moses Isserles, whose rulings are usually followed by Ashkenazic Jews, concurs with Rabbenu Tam.

34 A woman may not perform a religious circumcision

Although the code book, *Yoreh Deah* (264:1), permits a woman to circumcise the male child, most rabbinic authorities were reluctant to grant women this religious responsibility. These authorities, however, were in disagreement among themselves. Here is a sampling of views: A woman may perform the *brit milah* only where there is no qualified male to circumcise the child. Even in the absence of a qualified male, a woman may not perform the circumcision. Only one who has experienced circumcision may circumcise a child. If a woman has already circumcised a child, the *brit milah* is considered valid, but she is not permitted to perform this function from the outset.

The father of the child, if he is qualified, is required to circumcise his son. If not, the father invites a *mohel*, a person specially trained in both the theory and practice of religious circumcision. The *mohel*'s competence is generally certified by both medical and Jewish authorities, and he is trained in the laws pertaining to the rite. Not everyone agrees that a Jewish doctor may be appointed to circumcise the child even in the absence of a *mohel*. Generally, the Orthodox community rejects the appointment of a physician unless he is also a certified *mohel*.

Most non-Orthodox Jews will generally accept a physician where a *mohel* is unavailable, provided that the physician meets these standards: He must be Jewish; he must be acquainted with the significance and procedure of the *brit milah* ceremony; he must be sensitive to Jewish tradition. The physician recites the blessing immediately before the circumcision, and a rabbi, who supervises the ceremony, confers the Hebrew name upon the child.

For those who accept the services of a qualified physician to perform the *brit milah* in the absence of a *mohel*, there should be no objection to appointing a woman doctor to perform the *mitzvah*, provided that she is knowledgeable of and sensitive to the traditional requirements.

SABBATH AND HOLIDAYS
Some Misconceptions

35   It is preferable to light Sabbath Candles after dark than not at all

Working women whose jobs prevent them from arriving home before the Sabbath, especially during the winter months, often assume that they may light candles after dark. They wish to observe the meaningful tradition of kindling Sabbath lights, and they reason that the ends should justify the means: Better to light the candles at a later hour than not at all.

It is true that generally it is preferable to observe part of the Sabbath than to ignore it altogether. For example, no one would discourage a Jew who must work on the Sabbath day from reciting the Kiddush, blessing the children and singing Sabbath songs at the table on a Friday evening. Nevertheless, to kindle Sabbath candles—a religious act—after the Sabbath has arrived is contrary to the spirit and the letter of the law. One does not transgress an explicit law even though it may result in one's enjoying the Sabbath atmosphere that candles provide.

The question of whether means may be disregarded to achieve desirable ends is explicitly addressed in the Torah. In the Book of Exodus the Israelites are instructed to build a Sanctuary, but before the details of its construction are presented, the Israelites are reminded to observe the Sabbath: "You shall kindle no fire throughout your habitations on the Sabbath Day." The reason the Sabbath law is inserted before the laws of building the Sanctuary is to exhort the Israelites that the Sabbath must not be violated even for the sacred purpose of building a Holy Tabernacle.

A woman seriously asked if prior to her coming home her non-Jewish maid was permitted to light the candles before the Sabbath. The response should be obvious: The blessing recited immediately after kindling the Sabbath candles is as important as the act of lighting them. It would make little sense for a non-Jew to recite the blessing thanking God for "commanding *us* to kindle the Sabbath lights." The commandment was not given to members of the non-Jewish community.

It is appropriate that if there are children in the home before the Sabbath arrives, they should be instructed to light the Sabbath candles at the proper time, approximately twenty minutes before sundown.

36   Jewish law requires that all work be prohibited on the Sabbath

Anyone who takes the Bible literally may conclude that no kind of work is permitted on the Sabbath. The Torah appears to be explicit: "But the seventh day is the Sabbath unto the Lord your God, in it you shall do no manner of work" (Exod. 20:10).

However, the biblical command does not specify all the kinds of work that are forbidden other than kindling a flame, plowing, harvesting, reaping, gathering wood, etc. The Talmud further refines the definition of work prohibited on the Sabbath. The sages enumerate thirty-nine major and many other secondary classifications of work that constitute a violation of the Sabbath. Additionally, there are other categories of work that should be avoided because they are not in the spirit of Sabbath rest.

Since the description of the Sabbath in the Bible is found immediately before the construction of the Tabernacle, the rabbis concluded that there was a connection between the two: All categories of work performed on the Tabernacle were meant to be prohibited on the Sabbath.

The common belief that any manner of work is prohibited on the Sabbath is incorrect. Jewish law does not prohibit physical exertion on the Sabbath. An observant

Jew may walk up a steep hill not only to attend Synagogue but even without a destination. It is permitted to serve the Sabbath meal to family, friends or strangers even though serving and clearing the table entail considerable physical activity. It is permitted to lift furniture within one's home (called one's private domain) on the Sabbath.

By the same token, some minor activities that do not require strenuous activity are, nevertheless, avoided because they violate the spirit of the Sabbath or because they may lead to a major desecration of the Sabbath. For example, discussing business matters, reading business correspondence, or directly asking a non-Jew to do what is forbidden to a Jew on the Sabbath is not permissible. (In years past a *"shabbos goy"* would be asked before the Sabbath to come into the home of an observant Jewish family on the Sabbath to light the stove and perform other chores forbidden to the Jew. This questionable arrangement is practiced rarely in our day even among traditional Jews.) An observant Jew will not handle money nor enter a place of business even though these activities cannot be regarded as work requiring strenuous physical activity.

To find the underlying principle behind the various Sabbath prohibitions is not simple. It is apparent, however, that in enacting these laws the rabbis were more concerned with the intent than with the mere letter of the law. Therefore, any activity that violates the goal of Sabbath observance is unacceptable.

And what is the overall goal? To resuscitate oneself physically, spiritually, and emotionally every seventh day of the week the better to cope with the competitiveness and tension of the other six days. Abraham J. Heschel expressed the purpose of Sabbath observance in his own inimitable style: "Six days we seek to dominate the world, on the seventh day we try to dominate the self" (*The Sabbath*, p. 13).

37 Yom Kippur is the saddest day of the year

Yom Kippur is the most sacred and solemn day in the Jewish calendar but it is not a day of sadness or mourning. The origin of Yom Kippur is biblical, and we do not find in the entire Torah any law requiring a morbid mood in connection with this holiest of days. Although the Bible speaks of "practicing self-denial" on the Day of Atonement, the phrase was interpreted as a requirement to fast; nowhere is sadness prescribed.

It is the Ninth Day of Ab (Tisha Be-Ab), commemorating the destruction of the First and Second Temples, that is the saddest day of the Jewish year, not Yom Kippur which is a day of spiritual cleansing. "For on this day shall atonement be made for you to cleanse yourself; from all your sins shall you be clean before the Lord" (Lev. 16:30).

In ancient times on Yom Kippur the High Priest would hold a celebration for his friends when he entered the Holy of Holies in peace and left in peace without hindrance. It was even a day of festivity and rejoicing in one's atonement and forgiveness.

Rabban Simon ben Gamliel states that there were no more joyful festivals than the Fifteenth of Ab (marking the beginning of the vintage season in ancient Palestine) and Yom Kippur:

On these days the maidens of Jerusalem would go outdoors in borrowed white dresses, thus avoiding any embarrassment to maidens who had no dresses of their own. The maidens would dance in the vineyards and say, "Young man, lift your eyes and see what kind of maiden you should choose for yourself. Do not regard physical beauty but rather family background. Grace is deceitful, beauty is vain, only the woman who reveres the Lord shall be praised" (Taanit 4:8).

Traditionally the Torah portion dealing with forbidden marriages is still read on Yom Kippur afternoon in most synagogues. A cogent reason given for reading this selection was to warn eligible men against selecting brides prohibited by the Torah, since in the days of the Temple betrothals were announced on Yom Kippur afternoon.

In the Jewish tradition the wedding day resembles Yom Kippur. Just as Yom Kippur atones for sins, so marriage serves the purpose of achieving atonement. The bride and groom fast on that day; the groom recites the *viddui*, the Yom Kippur confessional. As it is the custom to wear white on the Day of Atonement to symbolize purity, so it is traditional for the bride to dress in a white gown and the bridegroom to wear a white robe (*kittel*).

With all its solemnity, Yom Kippur is also a holiday on which is recited the *sheheheyanu* (blessing of attainment), usually reserved for festive occasions.

38 *Kol Nidre* is the most important prayer recited on Yom Kippur

Kol Nidre is not a prayer at all. It is rather a declaration on behalf of the congregation that all vows pertaining to religious obligations that were not fulfilled during the past year or that may be broken in the coming year shall not be counted as binding.

In Mishnaic times a person who wished to annul a vow would appear before a court of three. On Yom Kippur Eve, when *Kol Nidre* is chanted, the leader of the service flanked by two men holding the scrolls is reminiscent of the court of three. *Kol Nidre* is intoned three times, again reminding us of the practice of reciting the legal formula of vow annulment three times. Because the *Kol Nidre* is similar to the court procedure, which could not be held on a holiday, it is recited before sundown. Thus, while it is yet light it is permitted to put on the *tallit*, not normally worn after dark, and to wear it throughout the entire evening Service.

Although the masses associate Yom Kippur with *Kol Nidre* more than with any other section of the liturgy, it was rejected by some prominent Jewish scholars, among them Saadya Gaon, Amram Gaon and Natronai Gaon. They saw no valid legal reason to recite this statement of absolution. Rabbi Amram went so far as to call the *Kol Nidre* a "foolish custom." And these objections were voiced *before* the present version of *Kol Nidre* was composed in the twelfth century in which Rabbenu Tam requested absolution not only of vows made in the year past but of future vows to be made "from this Yom Kippur until the next."

These vows do not refer to promises made to another person; they refer to religious vows made only to God. There is no formula for retracting business promises, yet anti-Semites over the centuries have cited the *Kol Nidre* as proof that Jews could not be trusted, that their promises and vows meant nothing to them. What is more, they were accused of dissolving their vows in advance before they were even uttered. This distrust was so intense in the pre-modern era that Jews were forced to take a special "Jew's Oath" in court. This degrading oath was abolished in Western Europe only after a few highly respected personalities—Moses Mendelsohn, Sir Moses Montefiore and others—strenuously fought against it.

The *Kol Nidre* held special meaning for Jews who were compelled to vow their loyalty to Christianity during the Spanish Inquisition (commencing in the latter part of the fifteenth century). They came secretly to the Synagogue on Yom Kippur to ask that their vows taken under duress be absolved, or to ask God's forgiveness for not yet returning to the Jewish faith despite their vows to do so.

The content of the *Kol Nidre* does not hold the same appeal that it did in centuries past, but the melody in which it is chanted continues to fill the worshipper with a feeling of awe and solemnity. The traditional melody, which is traced to the sixteenth century, has absorbed into it the agony of Jewish suffering and martyrdom.

39 A person who is ill may choose to eat on Yom Kippur

It is generally known that a person who is ill may eat on the Day of Atonement, when Jews are required to abstain from all nourishment. What is not common knowledge, however, is that he *must* eat on that day. Even if he wishes to fast in spite of his illness, he must follow the advice of his physician. Furthermore, if the patient claims that he cannot fast, his opinion is accepted even if his physician does not agree. "The heart alone knows its own bitterness" (Prov. 14:10).

A patient need not be gravely ill in order to eat and drink on Yom Kippur. Even where a question exists whether fasting would be detrimental to his health, he must not take that risk. Should his health deteriorate if he chooses to fast, he would be transgressing the principle of self-preservation. Time and again the biblical verse in Leviticus is cited and interpreted by the rabbis: "You shall keep My laws and My norms, by the pursuit of which *a man shall live*: I am the Lord." And the interpretation: He shall *live* by them, *and not die* by them (Yoma 85b).

A principle regarding transgressing the Sabbath in an emergency, may also apply to a patient taking nourishment on Yom Kippur: It is preferable to transgress a single Sabbath so as to observe many other Sabbaths in the future. Furthermore, in regard to medical treatment, the rabbis warned that those who are ill should not follow the principle that "whoever is more scrupulous is deserving of praise." They urge that in a case of illness it is a mitzvah to transgress Sabbath law. They even state that the sick may be compelled to accept treatment since unwillingness to be treated is a foolish brand of piety.

The sages deal with yet another problem. Granted that the patient must take food and drink on Yom Kippur, should he also recite the usual blessings before and after the meal? Their response is unequivocal; he is expected to recite the appropriate prayers and even include a phrase in the Grace After Meals referring to "this fast day of Yom Kippur."

The authorities also discuss the status of a woman who has given birth before Yom Kippur. For the first three days after birth she is regarded as one who is dangerously ill and is not permitted to fast. From the third to the seventh day she is considered as any other person who is ill and the same laws apply to her as to all patients. After that she normally is treated like any healthy person.

Children nine years old or younger must not be permitted to fast even if they wish to do so. Those older than nine should be trained to fast, gradually adding hours each year until they reach religious maturity.

40 Hanukkah is a major Jewish holiday

If the importance of a holiday were judged by the numbers of Jews who observed it, then Hanukkah should be regarded as a major festival. Present statistics reveal that more than three American Jews in four now light Hanukkah candles. Only Passover is more widely recognized, with nine Jews in ten reporting that they attend a *seder*.

Marshall Sklare, the eminent sociologist, suggests that the most popular rituals in Jewish life are those that meet five criteria: They can be redefined in contemporary terms; they do not require social isolation; they provide an alternative for Jews to a widely observed Christian holiday; they are centered on the children; they are not performed with great frequency.

Both holidays—Hanukkah and Passover—meet these criteria more than any of the other holidays in the Jewish calendar.

Nonetheless, the Jewish tradition does not regard Hanukkah as a major holy day of festival. There are basic criteria for such holidays that do not apply to Hanukkah: all the major holidays are mentioned in the Five Books of Moses; work is prohibited on all the major holidays; an elaborate liturgy is associated with the major Jewish holidays. Hanukkah, by contrast, originated after the Five Books of Moses were completed; normal work is permitted during the entire eight days of the festival; only a few appropriate prayers are inserted into the daily liturgy for Hanukkah.

Hanukkah is given limited space in the Talmud and is not even mentioned in the Mishna. The Talmudic discussion begins with the question, "What is Hanukkah?" It appears as if the answer was not very well known by the masses when the Talmud was written down in the fifth century.

Why is Hanukkah omitted from the Mishna? Rabbi Moses Sofer theorizes that the compiler of the Mishna, Rabbi Judah the Prince, deliberately omitted the Hanukkah story. His reasoning is that Rabbi Judah, who claimed to be a descendant of Kind David, regarded the Hasmoneans (a priestly family, usually referred to as the Maccabees) as usurpers since they did not descend from the line of King David and were not entitled to rule over Israel.

There is also a political reason suggested for omitting from the Mishna any mention of the Maccabees, who liberated Judea from the enemy. The Romans who ruled Judea during the period when the Mishna was compiled would have interpreted any emphasis on a Jewish war of independence as a call for rebellion against Rome as well, thus endangering the entire Jewish community. This theory might also explain why the Talmud does not mention the Maccabean military victories when it poses the question about the meaning of Hanukkah. The Talmud emphasizes only the spiritual significance of the holiday — the miracles of the cruse of oil and the rededication of the Temple.

Only with the rise of Jewish nationalism in recent times, has Hanukkah again become a popular holiday, with emphasis placed on the military and political victory of the Maccabees. The low-keyed observance of Hanukkah in the home and synagogue eventually took the form of public demonstrations. The military heroism of the Maccabees inspired a new feeling of nationalism among Eastern European Jews. This emphasis on the Maccabean victory reached its peak in modern Israel where Hanukkah is celebrated as a patriotic holiday.

The widespread observance of Hanukkah in Israel and the diaspora should be encouraged so long as it is still recognized as a minor Jewish festival. It is not on a par with the major Jewish festivals such as Sukkot and Shavuot, which are little observed by the majority of Jews.

41 Passover is primarily a child-centered holiday

It is true that a significant portion of the Passover *seder* involves the children in the household so that they will remember the Exodus from Egypt and, in turn, transmit the importance of this momentous event to their own children.

The four questions are asked to arouse the curiosity of the young. The account of the four sons was cleverly arranged by the rabbis so that the child would hope to identify himself with the wise son, not the irreverent, the simple or the silent son. The Passover songs are postponed to the end of the *seder* in order to encourage the young to remain awake after the sumptuous meal. Other techniques are also used to jog the memory of the younger generation and to create a mood that the child will anticipate long before the arrival of the holiday.

To claim that Passover is basically a child-centered holiday, however, may imply that the *seder* has little value if children are not present and that the *seder* ceremony need not be held for adults only. Jewish law is explicit on the need to observe the *seder* regardless of who is present at the table.

Maimonides in his *Mishneh Torah* elaborates on the Talmud's views regarding the adult's role at the *seder*:

If he has no son, his wife asks him [the questions]. If he has no wife then those present ask one another "Why is this night different?" even if they are all wise. If he is alone he asks *himself* the question, "Why is this night different?"

A familiar passage found in the Haggadah describes how five illustrious sages celebrated the *seder* in B'nai B'rak. They discussed the Exodus from Egypt throughout the night until they were interrupted by their students who reminded them that the time had arrived to recite the morning *shema*. It is apparent that their celebration of the *seder* was held on a highly sophisticated level which probably did not include their students.

Significantly the account of these five sages is mentioned to support the lesson that precedes it:

> Even if all of us were scholars, even if all of us were sages, even if all of us were elders, even if all of us were learned in the Torah, it would still be a duty to tell the story of the Exodus from Egypt.

Thus tradition does not regard the *seder* primarily as a child-centered ceremony in which adults *also* participate merely in order to instruct the young.

42 The Ten Commandments contain the essence of Judaism

The Ten Commandments are heard in the synagogue three times during the year; they are read from the Books of Exodus and Deuteronomy and are repeated on the festival of Shavuot, which commemorates the giving of the Torah at Mount Sinai. The worshippers are asked to rise for the reading of the Decalogue to highlight its special significance in Jewish history.

Given their importance, it is surprising that the Ten Commandments are not found in the religious service throughout the year. At one time they were part of the daily service. During the period of the Second Temple the Priests would recite the Decalogue at every morning service before the three biblical passages that comprise the *shema* section (Tamid 5:1). However, the recitation of the Decalogue was eventually removed from the daily service.

The Jerusalem Talmud (Berakhot 27a) provides the reason for the radical measure of removing the Ten Commandments from the liturgy: "So that the sectarians [early Christians] would not be able to claim that the Ten Commandments alone were revealed at Mount Sinai." The rabbis who were responsible for the change of format disputed the claim of the early Christians that God handed down only the Ten Commandments at Sinai. According to the rabbis, God revealed the entire written Torah as well as the Oral Torah—the future teachings of the rabbis.

Centuries later an earnest attempt was made by Babylonian rabbis to include the Ten Commandments in the liturgy once again. They were unsuccessful, however, since the custom not to read the Decalogue before the *shema* was long accepted as standard procedure. However, the rabbis emphasized that the essence of the Ten Commandments was to be found in the three paragraphs of the *shema* recited daily. For example, "Hear O Israel" reflects the first commandment, "I am the Lord Your God"; "The Lord is One" alludes to the second commandment, "You shall have no other gods before Me," etc.

By removing the Decalogue from the daily liturgy, the authorities were confronting a problem in their day which still persists among many well-meaning Jews who claim that the totality of Judaism is found in the Ten Commandments. These commandments represent only minimal moral requirements for the general community. They were never intended to serve as the sum total of one's responsibilities to God and man. Added to these basic commands are many other biblical laws which indicate in greater detail what God requires of man to maintain a viable society. Also, particularly for the Jew, the Decalogue does not include the requirement to observe any of the holy days other than the Sabbath. The many ritual observances found elsewhere in the Bible and the Talmud, but not in the Decalogue, are also an integral part of living as a committed Jew.

RITUAL PRACTICE
AND OBJECTS
A Closer Look

43 The observance of a Jewish custom is optional

When we speak of customs, we usually think of folkways developed over a long period of time that are not required to be followed by members of the community. Courteous customs such as the tipping of the hat or a handshake may be left to the discretion of the individual.

However, in Jewish life a *minhag*, or custom, which is not found in the Bible or Talmud can, nevertheless, assume the importance of law and is binding on the community where it is practiced. The Jewish sources remind us that "One must not change the custom" or "If you come into a city, guide yourself according to its customs." And occasionally, "Custom overrules law."

There are several reasons why customs were taken so seriously by the legal authorities. First there was a practical reason: If the rabbis attempted to abolish a cherished local custom that the community observed over a period of many years, they knew that the masses would probably continue to observe it over their protests. Therefore, so long as the custom did not transgress a biblical or Talmudic law, they permitted it, and at times reinforced it by incorporating it into the law. The second reason why many local customs took on legal status was based on an attitude of respect, if not awe, toward the community consisting of committed

Jews. The Latin aphorism that "the voice of the people is the voice of God" generally operated in Jewish life. Therefore, customs adopted by a "holy community" must have been sanctioned by God. Some of the folk customs that were eventually accepted as binding law are the son's recitation of the mourner's *kaddish* for eleven months, which originated in Germany in the thirteenth century; decorating the synagogue and home with flowers on Shavuot; eating dairy dishes on Shavuot; eating an apple dipped in honey on Rosh Hashanah; the tashlikh ceremony on Rosh Hashanah where prayers are recited by the river's edge to cast off one's sins.

Most of the differences in ritual between Ashkenazic and Sephardic Jews can be traced to the different customs adopted within these two communities. Their own local customs became legally binding for each community and both were required to remain faithful to their own customs without questioning the authenticity of the other's laws. For example, the custom among Sephardim of eating rice on Passover was regarded not as a liberal interpretation of the law, but rather as a law originating in Sephardic custom. By the same token, it is a law originating in custom among Ashkenazic Jews to refrain from rice on Passover. Both observances are correct and cannot be challenged, depending on the community with which one is affiliated.

In order for a *minhag* to become the accepted law, a highly respected rabbinical scholar had to endorse it. Especially in the Middle Ages several legal authorities undertook the task of determining which customs were necessary to strengthen the religious life of their communities. The most influential of these medieval Jewish authorities was Rabbi Jacob Molin, known as the *Maharil*. During the second half of the fourteenth and the beginning of the fifteenth centuries the *Maharil* set out to rebuild the Ashkenazic communities of Western Europe that had been weakened by persecution and the Black Death (1348-1349). By restoring the sanctity of the *minhag*, the *Maharil* was instrumental in revitalizing the religious life of Ashkenazic Jewry.

Some of the folk customs that the *Maharil* declared to be binding on Ashkenazim were stricter than the rabbinic laws. He reasoned that the masses were so uninformed and frivolous that to be lenient would result in unacceptable behavior. For example, he rejected the custom of writing theological poems in the vernacular. He also prohibited the custom of drinking wine at a circumcision ceremony during the week in which *Tisha Be-av* occurs.

On the other hand, he authorized many folk customs that were more lenient than the previous law. For example, he permitted a wedding ceremony to be held on Friday, he permitted men to work late in the afternoon on Fridays prior to the Sabbath, he allowed children to play games with nuts on the Sabbath, and he permitted young people to set fire to the branches of the *sukkah* on *Simhat Torah*.

44 In Jewish law a rabbi's presence is required at a wedding or funeral

In Talmudic times a *rav* or rabbi was not a professional, set apart from the layman, with special duties. He was primarily an interpreter and expounder of the Torah and the Oral Law. With few exceptions, the rabbi also engaged in another occupation in order to support his family. It was not until the beginning of the nineteenth century that the rabbi's formal duties consisted of leading the congregation in prayer and officiating at marriages and funerals.

In the original Jewish law marriage did not involve the civil government; it was a private transaction exclusively between the bride and groom. Thus the presence of an officiant is not technically required to validate the marriage. The Talmud merely requires an expert in Jewish law, who need not be a rabbi, to render decisions should legal problems arise regarding the marriage. However, to be certain that the laws of marriage were fulfilled, it was felt that a knowledgeable person should supervise the marriage procedure. The custom then evolved that a rabbi or his appointee act as the officiant.

In America marriage ceremonies were performed for many years by any person who conferred upon himself a religious title. The results were chaotic. In more recent years, however, most states have enacted laws requiring that only an ordained rabbi can officiate at a Jewish marriage ceremony. In some states cantors are also permitted to officiate at weddings.

Also, a rabbi's presence is not required to officiate at a funeral. A layman may be asked to recite appropriate psalms and to chant the Memorial Prayer. Nor must the eulogy be delivered by a rabbi. A member of the family or a friend of the deceased may eulogize the dead. At one time it was the custom to choose a speaker who was gifted with the power to evoke tears at the funeral. To weep over a pious person was regarded as a virtue, and one orator would compete with another to be chosen as the more emotional speaker.

Today most funeral services are conducted by rabbis, primarily because of their experience and professional skill, not because Jewish law requires them to lead the service.

In sum, a learned layman is legally permitted to conduct almost all the functions that the contemporary rabbi is now expected to perform on behalf of the community.

46   Jewish dietary laws were ordained for health reasons

It is not only the less educated Jews who have reasoned that the laws of *kashrut* were ordained for health reasons; some of the most prominent medieval authorities in seeking a rationale for the dietary laws associated them with preserving health.

For example, Rabbi Shmuel Ben Meir (twelfth cent.) exclaims: "All animals that God prohibited are offensive; they damage and inflame the body." Maimonides claims that the reason the pig is forbidden is that it is offensive, feeding itself on filthy things.

Now if swine were used for food, market places and even houses would have been dirtier than latrines. ... You know the saying of the sages, "The mouth of a pig is like walking excrement."

Nahmanides (thirteenth cent.) offers a health reason in differentiating between *kosher* and non-*kosher* fish. The fish with scales and fins are closer to the surface of the water, so they can come up for air, which warms their blood and thus helps them to rid their bodies of impurities. Those fish without fins and scales are dangerous to one's health.

Jewish tradition demands extreme care for our bodies and constant concern over our health. For this reason, good eating habits are emphasized. Gluttony is sharply denounced in the Torah and the rabbinic sources. We are encouraged to eat slowly and not to leave the dinner table abruptly. The meal should be accompanied by Torah discussion, which permits a more relaxed atmosphere.

It is this consistent health consciousness that may have contributed to the popular notion that the dietary laws were ordained primarily for hygienic reasons.

On further reflection, however, we cannot help but question the hygienic reasons behind the dietary laws. If hygiene were the primary reason for *kashrut*, then the ancient dietary laws would no longer be necessary now that food regulations are rigidly enforced. Long before health regulations were established, the great Spanish scholar Isaac Abarbanel stated that people who eat pork and insects are "well and alive and healthy to this very day." He rejects the health rationale for *kashrut* with these words:

> God forbid that I should believe the reason for forbidden foods to be medicinal! If it were so, the Book of God's Law would be in the same class as any of the minor brief medical books. ... The law of God did not come to heal bodies and seek their physical welfare but to seek the health of the soul and cure its illness.

Although the Torah and Talmud do not offer specific reasons behind the dietary laws, the goals are primarily nationalistic and moral.

First, by observing the laws of *kashrut* the Jews maintain their distinctiveness as a people. In differentiating between foods that are permitted and those that are prohibited, the Jewish community retains its uniqueness, thereby resisting assimilation.

The second goal of the dietary laws was to enable the Jew to achieve holiness. To our forbears holiness was not an elusive goal, but something real and attainable. By taking the common biological act of eating and elevating it into a religious act, the Jew achieved holiness in his daily routine.

The rabbis regarded eating of meat as a compromise that God made with man. Adam and Eve ate only vegetation (Gen. 1:27-29). Not until the time of Noah was meat permitted to man (Gen. 9:3-4). However, Noah and his family were required to follow certain humanitarian laws; they were prohibited from drinking blood or eating the limb torn from a live animal.

Later, the rabbis set up many more intricate laws so that before tasting the flesh of an animal, the Jew would become aware that he was deviating from the ideal of abstaining from meat altogether, for in order for one to eat meat the life of the animal must be taken.

The moral emphasis is further apparent in some of the specific laws of *kashrut*:

Animals that are permitted must be painlessly slaughtered by a knowledgeable and reverent Jew (*shohet*) who pronounces a blessing before taking the animal's life.

The blood of the slaughtered animal must be removed before it is eaten, since blood was deemed a symbol of life, another reminder that all God's creation should be treated with reverence. The sages believed that if blood were permitted, we would eventually become accustomed to the sight of blood, and even the shedding of human blood.

Commenting on the prohibition against eating blood, Jacob Milgrom has written that it even takes precedence over the Ten Commandments in the mind of the fathers of Judaism. The Hebrew Bible, even the Ten Commandments, were intended for Israel alone, but the prohibition against blood is commanded to all people. "Obviously, the Bible felt it more essential to a stable world than the Decalogue," says Milgrom. The Ten Commandments are merely a credo, but a law that seeks to curb the aggressive nature of man is doomed to fail unless "rooted and remembered in a regularly observed ritual, one which will intrude into the home, adhere to the family table, and impinge daily on the senses" (*Directions*, University of Judaism, 1981).

47 We may eat as much as we like if the food is *kosher*

If a person were searching for a biblical verse to sanction overeating, he could cite the following source from the Book of Deuteronomy:

> If the place where the Lord has chosen to establish His name is too far from you, you may slaughter any of the cattle or sheep that the Lord gives you, as I have instructed you; *and you may eat to your heart's content* in your settlements (Deut. 12:21).

True, the Bible does not place a limit on food intake, but there is always the danger of arriving at a generalization from a single verse in the Bible. The passage relating to the disloyal and defiant son, also found in Deuteronomy, refers to the sin of gluttony: "And they [his parents] shall say to the elders of the city: 'This our son is stubborn and rebellious, he does not hearken to our voice; *he is a glutton* and a drunkard'" (21:20). The Bible does not imply that he is eating unlawful food. He may be called a glutton even by gorging himself with acceptable food.

The whole problem of overeating along with excessive drinking must include the post-biblical views, which are more specific.

Ben Sirah says, "Eat, as it becomes a man, those things that are set before you, and devour not ... be not insatiable. When you sit among many people, do not be the first to reach out your hands."

Moses Maimonides, who advocated moderation as a philosophical and practical principle, cautions: "Gluttonous eating is comparable to consuming poison." To Maimonides causing harm to one's body was also a moral violation against God.

Elsewhere Maimonides directs himself to poor eating habits among scholars:

A scholar will not be a glutton but will eat food conducive to his health. Of such food he will not eat in excess. He will not be eager to fill his stomach like those who gorge themselves until the body swells. I refer to those who eat and drink all their days as if they were holidays. The wise will partake of only one or two courses. He will consume only as much as he needs to sustain himself.

Nahmanides (thirteenth cent.) also refers to the benefit of consuming wine and meat in moderation, but he warns against becoming "sordid within the boundaries of the Torah," eating and drinking to excess that which is permitted in moderation.

To summarize the Jewish objection to excessive eating, two basic principles were emphasized: First, we eat to live and we do not live to eat. Second, eating is regarded as a sacred act, *davar she-bikdushah*. Thus, the meal is surrounded by a prayer before we partake of food and the recitation of Grace after the meal. Even during the meal we are taught to discuss words of Torah so that the family is nourished not only by God-given food but by His *word* as well.

48 Judaism is not compatible with vegetarianism

Many traditional Jews believe that it is a religious requirement to celebrate the Sabbath and holidays by eating meat; otherwise the spirit of the holy day would not be fulfilled. They may refer to passages from the Talmud to support their views. "It is a transgression to abstain from that which the Torah permits" (Jerusalem Talmud Nedarim). Or "A man will have to justify himself in heaven as to why he did not eat the foods which he saw" (Kiddushin). Moses Maimonides in his Mishneh Torah also rebuked those who voluntarily abstained from eating meat. He equated them to extremists who choose to refrain from wine, from marriage, from dwelling in a decent home, or from wearing attractive clothing. "Whoever persists in such a course is termed a sinner" (Book of Knowledge, 3:1).

Most committed Jews never question the propriety of consuming meat. Some of the most popular Sabbath songs (*zemirot*) speak of the delights of eating meat in honor of the Sabbath. Less advantaged Jewish families refrained from eating meat during the week in order to purchase meat in honor of the Sabbath or holidays.

In recent years, however, a serious effort has been made to promote the vegetarian diet as another legitimate expression of authentic Judaism. Louis Berman, the author of *Vegetarianism and the Jewish Tradition*, supports the position of an observant Jewish vegetarian. He explains his view:

> Vegetarianism is for those who find spiritual satisfaction in "not eating things that breathe." Not everyone feels this way, and that is all right ... Motives for or against vegetarianism vary from person to person. For some the health motive is all-important. It is popular to look down on "health faddists," but in the Jewish tradition the preservation of life has a high ethical value (p. 66).

Rabbi Zalman Schachter indicates that our ancient ancestors were pastoral people. They raised animals for food; they drank liquids from leather flasks and wore clothes made from animal skins; they read from a Torah written on parchment, used the ram's horn as a shofar and said their morning prayers with tefillin (phylacteries). In light of our pastoral history it is remarkable, writes Schachter, that the Jews gave the world a story of Creation when Adam and Eve ate no meat, and a vision of the Messiah when "the lion will eat straw like the ox." Is this not an intimation that all the world would become vegetarian in the ideal future?

Some of the most celebrated Jewish personalities in recent times, religious and secular alike, were committed to the principle of vegetarianism. The widely respected Rabbi Abraham Isaac Kook, who served as religious leader of the Ashkenazic community in Palestine, vigorously supported vegetarianism. Kook explains the requirement to cover the slaughtered animal's blood with dust as hiding one's shame because we *should* feel guilt and shame for taking the life of a creature of God.

Kook disagreed with his critics who claimed that prohibiting meat consumption is a form of arrogance, as if we are superior to our ancestors who sharpened their knives to slaughter animals without feelings of guilt. Kook regards Jewish history as an evolutionary process from Genesis to Isaiah. He cites the words of the prophet Isaiah: "They will not do evil nor will they destroy anything in the entire mountain of my holiness because the knowledge of the Lord will fill the land as the waters cover the seas." According to Rabbi Kook, these prophetic words uttered by Isaiah indicate that man will eventually evolve spiritually to the point where he will no longer destroy animals even for food.

Kook also finds support for vegetarianism from the prophet Malachi: "And the meal offering of Judah and Jerusalem will be sweet unto the Lord as it was originally from the earliest years." Kook claims that the only sacrifice that will be acceptable in the Third Temple will be vegetarian — an allusion to the Garden of Eden, where meat was prohibited to Adam and Eve.

Are Jewish vegetarians suggesting that their tradition was wrong to encourage the eating of meat over the centuries? Not at all. They are more concerned with the health and moral factors of diet as it affects the present and future generations. Past generations cannot be held responsible for what they did not know about the findings of modern biochemistry. Nor are most religious vegetarians out to missionize among those who continue to include meat in their diet so long as their own life style is recognized as an authentic expression of Judaism.

49   The purpose of the *mezuzah* is to ward off evil

The *mezuzah* (literally, doorpost) consists of a metal, wood or ceramic container inside of which is a small roll of parchment. Handwritten on the parchment are the *shema*, which refers to the *mezuzah*, and two other biblical passages concerning the love for God and His precepts (Deut. 6:4-9; 11:13-21).

Affixing the *mezuzah* on the doorpost is one of the commandments that serves as a visual reminder of one's moral obligations. Maimonides observes that every time a Jewish person enters or leaves the home he will once again remember the love due to God and he will turn from the vanities of this world to choose the path of righteousness. Other authorities claim that the purpose of the *mezuzah* is to identify the Jewish home or to express the spirit of unity and solidarity wherever Jews live by means of this common symbol on the doorpost.

The *mezuzah* was never intended to serve as an amulet of protection from the forces of evil. Maimonides admonishes those who regard the *mezuzah* as an amulet or a lucky charm for the household; they are steeped in ignorance. He severely criticizes those who associate the *mezuzah* with magic and he claims that "they have no portion in the world to come." Not only do they fail to fulfill the commandment, but "they promote their own personal interests thinking that the *mezuzah* will secure for them an advantage in the vanities of the world."

Wearing the *mezuzah* as jewelry is not objectionable even without the prescribed parchment, so long as the wearer is aware that it does not contain protective powers against illness or mishaps. Like the Star of David or *hai* (*chai*), the *mezuzah* serves as a Jewish identification and nothing more. Similarly, a magnetic *mezuzah* on the dashboard of the automobile should not give the driver the security that he is immune to accidents or relieved from taking out auto insurance.

Today it is fashionable for some non-Jews to wear the *mezuzah* along with the crucifix, rabbit's foot, and other charms — just another indication of the widespread but distorted belief in the magical power of this religious object that was never meant to offer protection.

50 The *yarmulke* is to be treated as a holy object

Surprisingly there are only a few objects that are classified in Jewish law as holy: the Torah scroll, tefillin (phylacteries), the mezuzah and scrolls containing the prophets and writings. These objects all contain God's name and must not be carelessly discarded or destroyed. As a rule, they are buried in a Jewish cemetery when no longer usable.

Another group of religious objects, although referred to in the Torah, are not holy in themselves. These include the *sukkah* (booth), and *lulav* (palm branch), both used at Sukkot, and *shofar* (ram's horn). Professor Max Kadushin in *The Rabbinic Mind* indicates that these objects are classified by Jewish law as *tashmishey mitzvah*. They are essential to a particular rite and nothing more. Thus, they may be discarded when they may no longer be used.

The covering for the head—*yarmulke* or *kippah*—is not even mentioned by rabbinic sources along with those objects that may be discarded. Its importance as an object for religious use is of later origin.

The only mention of head attire in the Torah is found in the Book of Exodus where Moses makes a head covering for the sons of Aaron. In Talmudic times wearing a head covering in Palestine was initially limited to rabbis, priests and scholars to signify their piety and knowledge. In Babylonia wearing a covering for the head was indicative of social and religious esteem. Rabbi Huna would never walk more than four cubits with an uncovered head, a practice that he learned from his mentor, Rav, one of the major personalities of the Talmud.

According to one theory, the Babylonian Jews probably brought with them the custom of wearing a head covering as they migrated through the Middle East, into North Africa and Spain (*Sepharad*). By the eleventh century the eminent Spanish scholar Moses Maimonides regarded the wearing of a head covering as a religious obligation.

The Jews of Palestine, however, who migrated north of the Mediterranean as far as Germany (*Ashkenaz*), limited the wearing of the hat to rabbis and other scholars and then only for special religious occasions.

After the Spanish Inquisition in 1492 a substantial number of Sephardic Jews were forced to find a new home in the Ashkenazic areas of Europe. They probably carried with them their widely observed tradition of regularly covering the head and thus influenced the Ashkenazic Jews to follow their example.

It was not until the nineteenth century that the custom of covering the head became a legal requirement for observant Jews. In reaction to the Enlightenment, which attracted the liberal Jews, the rabbinate wanted to create a visible distinction between the observant and those who sought to liberate themselves from Jewish traditions. By requiring the head to be covered at all times, the traditionalists sought to maintain a separate identity from the liberal Jews and the Gentile majority as well.

Although the *yarmulke* is worn with pride throughout the day by observant Jews, its widespread use does not confer holiness on the object itself. It may be discarded like any other article of clothing.

51   The Star of David is a
sacred symbol that should be
displayed in every synagogue

Only two religious symbols are found in every synagogue, the Holy Ark in which the Torah Scrolls are kept
and the Eternal Light, Even the *menorah* (candela-
brum), although it may be seen in many synagogues
throughout the world and is of biblical origin, is not required to be placed in a House of Worship.

Most synagogues display the Star of David, the *magen David*, as an art form either within the Sanctuary or
on the exterior of the building. Yet this symbol does not
contain any special religious significance. It serves only
to give a Jewish identification to a building. The Star of
David is not required to be displayed.

We cannot be certain when Jews began to use the
six-pointed star for the first time. During the era of the
Second Temple, the six-pointed star was frequently displayed by both Jews and non-Jews along with the five-
pointed star. In the ancient synagogue of Capernaum
(second or third century C.E.) the six-pointed star is
found side by side with the five-pointed star on a frieze.
Scholars assume, however, that it was used for a decora-
tive purpose only without religious significance.

It was not until the fourteenth century that the six-
pointed star becomes known by a special name — the

Shield of David. Professor Gershom Scholem suggests the specific year of 1354, when Charles IV permitted the Jewish community of Prague to bear its own flag, later called in documents "King David's Flag." On this flag was found the six-pointed star. This hexagram then became the official emblem of the Prague Jewish community, probably chosen as a proud symbol of the ancient past when King David allegedly wore the star on his shield. This explains the beginning of its use in synagogues, on printed books and on other objects among the Prague community.

Not until the nineteenth century, however, was the *magen David* widely used by European Jewish communities. Scholem contends that the primary reason for the popularity of the six-pointed star among Jews was that it served as a "striking and simple sign which would 'symbolize' Judaism in the same way as the cross symbolized Christianity." In time most synagogues began to use the symbol; many communities with their charitable organizations stamped it on their seals and letterheads.

At the turn of the century the Zionist movement under Herzl's leadership adopted the *magen David* as a sign of hope and a new future for the Jewish people. It became the symbol on the Zionist flag and in 1948 was adopted as the official emblem on the flag of Israel.

The spiritual significance of the *magen David* may be attributed to its use as a marker identifying those buried in Jewish cemeteries and to its association with the Holocaust when the Nazis required it to be worn by Jews as a badge of shame. In defiance, the survivors conferred a positive meaning on the *magen David*. They associated it with a renewed pride in their ancestry and faith in its eternal message.

PRAYER
Correcting Some Impressions

52 Prayer is essentially asking something of God

Many people associate prayer exclusively with requesting favors of God. That is not surprising. The English world *prayer* has its origin in the Latin verb *precare* meaning to beg or entreat; the German word for prayer *gebet*, connotes the same meaning. Despite this widespread belief that prayer means petition, many Jews find it difficult to ask God for things or for special favors. They prefer to help themselves or to ask a friend to help them and not to rely on a God whose existence is concealed in mystery.

The Jewish concept of prayer certainly includes petitioning God for health, sustenance and other favorable things, but Jews maintain that there are higher degrees of prayer than petition. The Hebrew verb "to pray" comes from a root meaning "to judge." It is probable that the original meaning was to judge or examine oneself in the presence of God, which remains an essential function of prayer. Many of the prayers that Jews recite during the High Holy Days are intended to help us examine who we really are. What is the direction of our lives and how can we get back on the right track? Those prayers that encourage self-examination in God's presence have greater spiritual value than prayers of petition.

The many prayers of appreciation take precedence over petitional prayers. The worshipper is encouraged to thank God for the daily blessings that can so easily be taken for granted. Gratitude is expressed through prayers offered before and after a meal. Prayers of appreciation are uttered daily for God's ongoing gifts found in nature. The Jew also expresses thanks for having received the Torah and the commandments.

It is significant that the thirteen petitional blessings recited in the daily *amidah* (silent devotion) are removed from the Sabbath *amidah* and are replaced with a single blessing expressing gratitude for the Sabbath (*mekadesh hashabbat*). The rabbis felt that the usual prayers of petition were not in keeping with the spirit of the Sabbath.

Even those petitional prayers recited during the week are recited in the plural so that the worshipper asks not merely for himself but for the entire community as well. It is also understood that petitional prayers require more than merely asking for God's performance. The worshipper is expected to cooperate with God in implementing the request.

In sum, petitional prayers are not discouraged so long as they represent a legitimate need. Prayers of request, however valid they may be, are less commendable than prayers of self-examination, gratitude, or affirmation of those moral values that God requires of the worshipper.

53 Personal meditation serves the same purpose as public prayer

Much has been written in Jewish sources, both classical and modern, about the importance of personal meditation as a value in itself and also as preparation for reciting the fixed prayers. In earlier times, pious men would sit in silence for an hour before prayer "that they might direct their heart toward God" (Berakhot 5:1).

Prayer is more than private meditation, however. Jewish tradition emphasizes the necessity to pray with and as part of the congregation. Judaism places a higher priority on community worship than on private prayer.

A midrash expresses this priority given to public worship. The Holy One said to the community of Israel: I have taught you to pray in the synagogues of your cities. But if you are not able to pray in the synagogues, you may pray in your homes. If you are unable to pray in your homes, you may pray in your beds. If you are unable to pray in your beds, then meditate in your hearts. For this is the meaning of the verse in Psalms (4:5), "Commune with your heart ... and be still" (Midrash on Psalms).

Jewish worship is essentially centered on community needs with a standardized liturgy for all worshippers to follow. Samuel, a third century scholar, formulated the rule that even when one prays for himself, he should include the entire community in the words of his prayer.

Abraham Heschel advocated personal prayer and also reminded us that "the Jew does not stand alone before God; it is as a member of the community that he stands before God. Our relationship to Him is not as an I to a Thou, but as a We to a Thou."

The value of private meditation, however, should not be underestimated. It helps the worshipper to concentrate more intensely on his relationship to God and man; it encourages spontaneity and creativity in prayer which is often absent when we recite routine prayers written by others. Thus, in order for one to maintain the sensitive balance of personal involvement in prayer and concern for the community, both personal and congregational prayers are valued in the Jewish tradition.

54 Translations of the Torah and the prayerbook are a concession to modernity

Translating the Torah into the vernacular was a Jewish practice as far back as the first century. Most Jews then did not speak Hebrew. In Palestine and Babylonia they spoke Aramaic, and in Egypt Greek was the spoken language.

In Palestine it was the custom, when calling up a person to read from the Torah, to call up a translator (*meturgeman*) as well. The reading from the Torah and the translation were presented verse by verse. The translator was not permitted to have written notes before him since the translation was regarded as part of the Oral Torah. He was not permitted to give a word-by-word translation nor to elaborate on the text. He was required to give a free but correct translation of the Torah text as it was being read. If he took liberties with his translation he was "silenced and admonished." One scholar sounds this warning: "He who translates a verse too literally is a falsifier; he who makes additions to it is a blasphemer."

As for praying in the vernacular, some teachers in Talmudic times resisted the practice. They believed that sacred prayers should be offered only in Hebrew, the holy tongue. These rabbis went so far as to resist the use of Aramaic prayers although Aramaic was regarded as a semi-holy language since portions of the Bible are in Aramaic. Rabbi Yohanan warns that if anyone prays for his needs in Aramaic, the Ministering Angels do not heed his prayers for they do not understand that language and therefore cannot deliver these prayers before God's throne. Nevertheless, prayer recited in the vernacular was not prohibited. Several Aramaic prayers, such as the *kaddish*, were introduced into the liturgy in the original Aaramaic instead of the Hebrew, and are still recited daily and on the Sabbath. Furthermore, the Mishna ruled that the *shema* and the *tefillah* (silent devotion) may be recited in any language that is familiar to the worshipper.

The first authentic translation of the *siddur* (Jewish prayerbook) into English dates back to the year 1766, when Isaac Pinto published his text in New York City for the benefit of the Sephardic Jews of London. However, his translation was not approved. Pinto then brought his English text to the colonies in the New World, where it was accepted by the Shearith Israel Congregation in New York.

Many translations of the *siddur* were published in the nineteenth century—in German, Italian, Polish, Spanish, Hungarian and other languages. Contrary to popular belief, translation into the vernacular is not a recent innovation to serve the needs of the contemporary American Jewish community.

RELATING TO
THE NON-JEWISH
COMMUNITY
Another Look

55 Jews have always discouraged converts

The authors of the Mishna formulated specific questions to be asked of a non-Jew seeking conversion: "What is your objective? Do you know that today the people of Israel are wretched, driven about, exiled, and in constant suffering?" On the basis of this text in the Talmud it would appear that Judaism discouraged proselytes and accepted them only with great reluctance.

However, other sources indicate that Jews welcomed and even actively sought converts. The New Testament (the title should not be understood as a completion of the Hebrew Bible) refers to the Pharisees who "compass sea and land to make one proselyte" (Matthew 23:15). Hillel, unlike his contemporary Shammai, was receptive to teaching potential converts the essentials of Judaism.

The Talmud records statements for and against conversion. Some scholars were suspicious of converts and their motives. An extreme view: "Proselytes are as difficult for Israel as a sore," is a generalization probably based on negative experiences with some converts. On the other hand, the Talmud also records views praising converts: "Proselytes are beloved; in every place He considers them part of Israel." Rabbi Eleazar and Rabbi Yohanan both claimed that "the Holy One,

Blessed be He, exiled Israel among the nations only in order to increase their numbers with the addition of proselytes." The tendency to enhance the reputation of proselytes and to encourage converts to Judaism may be found in tracing the origins of great sages such as Rabbi Meir and Rabbi Akiba to their non-Jewish ancestry.

Though Jews were active missionaries at one time, they never conceived their historic mission as being to convert the world or to engage in a holy war to convert infidels to Jewish belief. The rabbis frowned upon forcible conversion. The only instances of forcible conversions took place under John Hyrcanus and his son, who coerced the Edomites and Ituraeans to accept Judaism in the second century before the Common Era. Hyrcanus's actions brought him into a bitter clash with the Pharisees, who did not even permit the forcible conversion of slaves to Judaism.

With the ascension of Constantine to the Roman Throne (312 C.E.) Jews were no longer permitted to engage in missionary activity. Constantine adopted Christianity as the state religion and placed restrictions on Jewish activities, including the ban on proselytizing. He demanded the death penalty for any person converting to Judaism. In response to his edict, the number of converts to Judaism diminished in Christian countries.

56 Converts to Judaism are like "second class citizens"

Once a proselyte accepts the responsibilities of living a full Jewish life, he becomes a *yisrael lekhol davar*, "an Israelite in every sense." Members of the Jewish community are warned not to remind the convert of his origins in a way that would be demeaning to the Jew by choice.

Maimonides responded to the proselyte Obadiah who wanted to know if he could recite the same prayers as those who were born Jews. He reminded Obadiah that converts to Judaism enjoy total equality and are, in fact, deserving of special love. In response to Obadiah's specific questions, Maimonides encouraged him to recite such blessings as "Who has chosen *us*," "Who has given *us*," "Who has taken *us* for Your own" and "Who has distinguished *us*." He goes a step further in reminding Obadiah that those who are born Jews are the descendants of Abraham, Isaac and Jacob, whereas the true convert is a direct descendant from God. He cites the biblical verse: "One shall say, I am the Lord's and another shall call himself by the name of Jacob" (Is. 44:5).

The only distinction that is made today between a born Jew and a convert is in religious documents where reference is made to the Hebrew name. Since the convert is regarded as "a newly born child" in the religious sense, he or she is referred to as the son or daughter of *Avraham Avinu*, "Our Father Abraham."

In Talmudic times some distinctions were made between a born Jew and a proselyte. The proselyte was not appointed to public office, and did not hold the office of judge in a criminal court but could judge in a civil court. Some authorities ruled that even in a civil court he could sit in judgment only over another proselyte. These distinctions do not exist today.

57 One who adopts another religion is no longer a Jew

The question as to whether the child of a Jewish mother or a convert to Judaism can ever shed his Jewish identity has been the subject of much discussion among scholars. Legally it is impossible for a Jew to cease being a Jew. The *halakhah* (Jewish law, lit.: "path" or "way") still regards the apostate as a Jew even if he openly embraces another faith. Although he is called a sinner for having alienated himself from Judaism, "A Jew even if he has sinned, remains a Jew" (Sanhedrin 44a). Nahmanides cites the verse from Deuteronomy (29:13-14) as support of this view: "I make this covenant with its sanctions, not with you alone, but both with those who are standing here with us today before the Lord our God and with those who are not with us here today." Thus, for both the born Jew and the proselyte, Jewish identity is no longer a matter of personal choice.

Professor Robert Gordis offers two basic reasons for this Jewish view of apostasy. First, many if not most who converted from Judaism in the past did so because they were threatened with physical punishment otherwise or were promised material advantages by accepting the dominant faith. The Jewish community continued to hope that deserters would eventually return, and so the door was left open for them. Second, the marriage bond was basic to Judaism. "The entire structure would be seriously weakened if the bond between husband and wife were to be declared null and void because a Jew had converted to another faith" (*Judaism in a Christian World*).

Because the apostate never leaves Judaism in the eyes of the Jewish law, he is not technically required to undergo a special ritual if he wishes to return to his former religion. Nevertheless, some authorities do require a tangible act to symbolize his return. He is asked to confess his transgressions before a court of rabbis and then to reaffirm his commitment to the laws of Judaism. Other authorities require ritual immersion in the same manner as the convert to Judaism.

Jews who were coerced to accept another religion out of fear for their lives are automatically accepted into the Jewish community merely by expressing their desire to return.

Even though the apostate technically remains a Jew for the remainder of his life, a Jew who voluntarily accepts another religion is regarded in some aspects *as though* he were no longer a Jew. This hostile feeling against the apostate is reflected in the law. For example, he is not reliable as a witness because he has renounced the Torah. A Jewish court could deny the apostate his father's inheritance. Also, mourning is not observed by Jewish relatives upon the death of an apostate.

58 Jews may not read or study from the New Testament

Some Jews refuse to read the New Testament since many of its passages are alien to the Jewish spirit. This reluctance may stem from an old tradition that Jews should not take an oath on the New Testament or that they may not utter the name of Jesus when referring to the founder of Christianity.

Indeed, attempts were made to discourage the reading of certain books as far back as the Mishnaic period (second cent.) when Rabbi Akiba prohibited Jews from reading the Apocrypha (a collection of books excluded from the canon of the Hebrew Bible). He claimed that Jews who choose to read these "external books" are denied a share in the world to come. The prohibition, however, was restricted to reading them publicly, thus giving non-sacred books the same attention as the sacred literature of the Hebrew Bible; there was no restriction against reading these books privately.

The rabbis also voiced opposition to the reading of books written in Greek. They feared the growing Hellenization among Jews population. The Books of the *Minim* — the early Christians and other sectarians — were also frowned upon by the religious authorities.

In the Middle Ages Maimonides restricted the reading of literature dealing with idolatrous worship, yet he himself read the current literature on idolatrous customs and astrology. His rationale was that it was important to understand how the Torah responded to the challenge of idolatry. Maimonides held a different standard for the masses and the scholars.

If the New Testament were a closed book to Jewish scholars or students, then it would not be possible to compare the basic ideas and insights found in the Hebrew Bible and the New Testament. We would not be able to refute some of the accusations made against the Pharisees. Jews would have to depend on non-Jews to digest the New Testament for them without having access to the source book of Christianity. The Jewish community has produced a group of first-rate scholars in recent years who have thoroughly studied and analyzed Christian literary sources. Fortunately, they were not inhibited from examining the New Testament.

59   The Pharisees were self-righteous hypocrites

Unfortunately, many dictionaries continue to define Pharisee erroneously as a hypocrite or sanctimonious person, on the basis of accusations found primarily in the Gospel according to Matthew (23). Jesus is quoted as having denounced the Pharisees as "hypocrites," "serpents," and "brood of vipers," who are certain to be sentenced to hell.

Objective scholars of the New Testament have expressed skepticism regarding whether these denunciations against the Pharisees were expressed by Jesus himself. Most likely they were wrongly attributed to Jesus by the writers of the Gospels who lived after Jesus during a time when hostility of Christians toward Jews became intense. Yet, many people continue to use the words "Pharisee" and "hypocrite" interchangeably, without understanding who the Pharisees were and what their historic role was in Jewish history.

During the Maccabean period, the *perushim* or Pharisees were a group of learned and observant Jews who interpreted the written Torah so that it could be better understood and followed by their contemporaries. To them, the Torah was a living instrument; its words could not be taken literally, as fundamentalists like the Sadducees insisted upon doing in their reading of Torah.

The Pharisees, then, expounded on the text with new clarifications and with new ethical concepts that they believed were intended originally by the Torah although not always expressed in the original text. For example, they emphasized belief in the immortality of the soul and the resurrection although these concepts are not explicitly found anywhere in the Five Books of Moses. They also liberalized some of the criminal laws found in the Torah For example, the biblical law, "An eye for an eye and a tooth for a tooth" (Exod. 21:24-25) was interpreted by the Pharisees to require only a monetary fine as penalty for inflicting physical injury.

The Pharisees also attempted to introduce greater equality into Jewish life by breaking down the barriers between the priest and the laity. For example, the Torah requires only the priests to be in a state of purity before partaking of sanctified food. The Pharisees and the early rabbis went further, requiring *all* Israelites to wash their hands even when eating ordinary food. They regarded this law as a divine commandment even though it is not found in the Scripture. For the Pharisees the whole people of Israel was to be "a kingdom of priests and a holy nation."

In sum, the Pharisees firmly believed that the words of the written Torah had to be supplemented by an expanded meaning of the original text as a response to the religious needs of their generation.

To be sure, not all the Pharisees were models of ethical behavior. Even the Talmud criticizes the false piety, the insincerity of certain members of this fellowship. But the moral failure of a small minority, does not warrant stigmatization of the entire Pharisaic tradition.

Classical Christian scholars—Herbert Danby, R. Travers Herford, George Foot Moore, and a great many others—were profoundly interested in the history of the Pharisees and have helped to vindicate them against the false accusations that were found in the New Testament and by subsequent generations of Christian theologians. In his scholarly work, *The Pharisees*, Herford emphasizes that the rabbis of the Talmud were the heirs of the Pharisees. Without the principles set down by the Pharisees, the works of rabbinic Judaism would not have emerged as the great creative achievement that it became.

> They had their faults—who has not? Their system was not perfect. ... But they did their work in their day, in spite of the sneers and ill-will of the Gentiles; the rabbis carried on what the Pharisees had begun and, through the labours of both, Judaism was carried safely down the ages (p. 238).

60   Traditional Jews are required to resist non-Jewish influences

The Torah is specific in warning the ancient Israelites to resist the influence of the Canaanites and other foreigners with whom they came into contact. The Talmud as well was aware of the danger of studying "Greek Wisdom," which the Jew was permitted to study only when "it is neither day nor night."

Despite these cautions, throughout Jewish history Judaism came under the influence of external cultures which helped to stimulate Jewish creativity. Although these encounters with other cultures exposed the Jews to the dangers of assimilation, Jews also enriched their own civilization by absorbing new ideas and insights from others. If the Jewish community had insisted on insulating itself from outside influences, it would have lost its vitality and its ability to confront new challenges in each stage of its development. These confrontations with the outside world saved the Jews from becoming just another sect.

Dr. Trude Weiss-Rosmarin has written extensively on this subject. She claims that, contrary to popular belief, assimilation is not always negative. Throughout their long history, Jews assimilated *from* majority cultures without assimilating *to* them. "Assimilation *to*" implies the loss of one's own culture; "assimilation *from*" helps to expand and enrich one's own culture by adapting the foreign culture, including its language, to the original culture of the Jews.

In spite of the warning against accepting Greek ideas, Jewish scholars used Greek words freely in the Talmud to describe what could not be precisely expressed in Hebrew or Aramaic. It is estimated that some three thousand Latin or Greek words can be found in Talmudic literature. These are Hellenistic words borrowed from areas such as commerce, music, folklore, the arts, geography, etc.

Medicine is well represented by Greek terms describing ailments and remedies. This long list of borrowed words and names offers a clear indication of the Greek influence on the culture of the Jews during the Talmudic era.

Dr. Samuel Sandmel has suggested that the Jews may have borrowed the elaborate use of wine in its rituals from the Greeks. There is no biblical basis for using wine at the wedding ceremony, at a circumcision, or at the beginning and end of the Sabbath. The Jews resisted borrowing from the Greeks, however, where borrowing meant compromising the essence of Judaism. For example, they would not accept idols, worship the Emperor or make the Olympian pantheon part of their religion. They learned what and how to adapt from their neighbors and were able to resist any foreign influence that would jeopardize Jewish survival

In Muslim Spain, commencing with the eighth century, the Jewish community entered into their "Golden Age," an era of unprecedented literary creativity. Some of the great Hebrew poets, Ibn Gabirol, Al-Harizi and Judah Halevi, were greatly influenced by Arabic poetic forms and imagery. Large numbers of Jews acquainted themselves with Muslim poetry, biography and history. The vocabulary of the Islamic faith is reflected in books written by Jews. Jewish writers refer to works of Arab scientists, philosophers and theologians.

Among the most prominent Spainish biblical commentators, the Arabic influence was very apparent. Abraham Ibn Ezra frequently explained biblical passages by referring to Arabic grammar. Nahmanides was likewise influenced by his knowledge of Arabic studies.

Maimonides, who is generally regarded as the greatest Jewish intellectual, wrote almost all of his works in Arabic. His *Guide for the Perplexed*, in which he attempts to reconcile reason and faith, is filled with references to the Muslim philosophers who captured the attention of the Jewish intellectuals of his day.

Maimonides goes to great lengths to analyze Aristotle's philosophy, describing his agreements and disagreements with Greece's most celebrated philosopher.

Since Aristotle's works were widely known and respected by the Muslim and Jewish contemporaries of Maimonides, Maimonides felt compelled to indicate where Judaism differed with the Greek philosopher, especially on the question of creation. Maimonides states that the belief in God's creation of the world "out of nothing" is crucial to Jewish belief; he rejects Aristotle's theory that the world was eternal without a divinely created act. Maimonides felt that a believing Jew could accept much of Aristotle's philosophy without jeopardizing his Jewish beliefs, but on the question of creation the Jew had to rely on faith regarding the biblical version of creation. Here we have a classic example of the ability of the Jew to adapt ideas from another culture without surrendering the essence of Jewish belief.

In our day we look upon the *hasidim* as the group most resistant to outside influences. Their closely knit community life, their admonition against higher secular education or watching television in order to minimize contacts with the non-Jewish world, are impressed on their followers.

In *The Jewish Mind,* the noted anthropologist Raphael Patai contends that the early *hasidim* borrowed very heavily from their Eastern European neighbors.

The tendency to adopt songs and dances from the Gentiles had been manifested by the Besht (founder of *hasidism*); subsequently his descendants, disciples and successors followed the example of the founder.

Patai indicates that many of the folk stories about kings, beautiful princesses, magnificent palaces, forests infested with bandits and wild beasts, and the like were all favorite themes in Ukranian folklore. The "Courts" of the *hasidic* rabbis resembled the Courts of Gentile high nobility, with their luxury, sumptuous clothing, fine food and drink. Furthermore, Patai theorizes that the hierarchical structure of the Polish Catholic Church can be seen in the ranking order among the *hasidic* Rabbis, something alien to traditional Judaism.

Even if some of these influences on *hasidism* from their neighbors stand to be refuted, it would be difficult totally to dismiss as an accident the similarities between the two societies. To accept the theory that Jews could hardly help but adopt certain ideas and institutions from their surroundings is to understand how new movements and new forms of expression developed within Judaism. The ability of the Jews to take these external influences and transform them into an authentic Jewish expression has been aptly described as the collective genius of the Jewish people.

61 Non-Jews may not be invited to a *seder*

Some Jews are reluctant to invite non-Jewish friends to a *seder* on Passover because they were told that it is contrary to Jewish tradition. Their reluctance may stem from several sources.

The Torah, in referring to the law of the Passover offering, states that the sacrificial meal may be eaten only by Israelites. "No foreigner shall eat of it. ... No uncircumcised person may partake of it" (Exod. 12). Since Jews no longer offer sacrifices or partake of a sacrificial meal, the biblical law is no longer applicable. True, the shankbone that is placed on the *seder* plate is a visual reminder of the ancient sacrificial offering, but it is only a symbolic object used as a visual aid for the participants seated around the *seder* table. It is not ritually eaten.

There is probably another more compelling reason why some Jews grew up with the assumption that non-Jews may not attend their *seder*. Frequently Passover coincides with Easter. For centuries the Easter holiday, associated with the crucifixion of Jesus, was a critical period for the Jews of Central and Eastern Europe. In their churches Christians listened to inflammatory sermons accusing the Jews of responsibility for the death of Jesus. Jews were also sometimes accused of killing

Christian children and using their blood to bake *matzot* for Passover. Some of the most infamous pogroms coincided with the Passover and Easter season. Because of the highly charged atmosphere at this season of the year, Jews were warned by their community leaders to remain inside their homes so as not to be exposed to their accusers. It is only natural then that most European Jews would not think seriously of inviting a Christian to their *seder*. This fear and reluctance lingered for many years even among Jews who came to America.

Since there is no legal prohibition against inviting non-Jews to a *seder*, Jews who feel more secure than their ancestors about their relationship with contemporary Christians need not feel any hesitation inviting their neighbors and friends to attend their family *seder*. The experience may enlighten such guests, helping them to understand why the *seder* continues to be observed with such fervor by most Jewish families; they will learn the significance of the various rituals at the table and will also discover some of the universal themes found in the Haggadah as they apply to all people who value freedom; they will observe how the origin of their major holiday of Easter was influenced by the more ancient festival of Passover.

62 A Jew may not offer prayers on behalf of a non-Jew

Many people are under the assumption that Jewish law forbids non-Jews to participate in any activity that takes place in a synagogue or that prayers may not be recited on their behalf.

Both assumptions are untrue. For example, a non-Jew is permitted to participate in a Jewish wedding held either in or outside of the Synagogue. A non-Jew may serve as an usher and even as best man or maid of honor at a Jewish wedding. These honors have no religious significance. They are primarily social. Similarly, at a Jewish funeral a non-Jew may also be asked to serve as a pall-bearer.

The question as to whether a non-Jew may handle a Torah scroll in the Synagogue has been answered in the affirmative by Moses Maimonides, who wrote that any person may hold a Torah scroll and even read from it, including a non-Jew. (Understandably, a non-Jew may not perform the *mitzvah* of reading from the Torah scroll at a religious service).

Regarding the recitation of prayers on behalf of a non-Jew, no legal objection may be found in Jewish sources. In fact, most standard prayer books include a special prayer for the heads of government in one's country regardless of their religious background.

A prayer may also be offered for a non-Jewish friend who is ill. It is not customary to recite a prayer for recovery publicly when the Torah is being read, since the Hebrew name is mentioned in the format of the prayer. However, a personal prayer during the silent devotion or at another time during the service may be offered for a non-Jew. A prayer for his or her recovery should be encouraged *mipney darkey shalom*, in order to promote harmony among different groups of people and to emphasize God's concern for all His children, regardless of their religious or social origin.

In a Responsum, Solomon Freehof cites the legal scholar Moses Isserles (sixteenth cent.), who was asked whether a son should recite the Mourner's *kaddish* for an apostate father. He responded that the son should recite the *kaddish* if the father who abandoned Judaism was slain but not if he died a natural death. Isserles reasoned that the slaying was a "means to atonement," for the father certainly would have repented before he was slain. This appears to be the prevailing opinion, yet another, less eminent scholar, Solomon Eiger, writes that if the apostate father has left no other mourners, then the son should recite *kaddish* for him even if his father died naturally.

Freehof then confronts the question as to whether one may say *kaddish* for a Christian. Freehof cites the responsum of Aaron Walkin (written in 1933). A man converted to Judaism, but his father did not convert. After the father's death the son wanted to say *kaddish* for his Gentile father. Aaron Walkin decided that he may. Walkin's reasoning is that if a son may say *kaddish* for an apostate father who abandoned Judaism, he may say *kaddish* for his father who naturally followed the religion in which he was brought up.

In theory a convert to Judaism is regarded as a newborn who has no kin and consequently has no religious responsibilities to those who were his kin before his conversion. However, the rabbis permit him to recite *kaddish*. Some authorities, including Walkin, suggest that it is his responsibility to do so. The same general rule applies to the recitation of *yizkor*, the memorial prayer that is recited on most major Jewish holidays.

DEATH AND MOURNING
Questioning What We Were Told

63 A Jew must not pray for the death of a person who is about to die

Since Judaism places such emphasis on preserving life at all costs, it is not generally known that a prayer may be offered that God release an incurably ill patient from his agony.

The Talmud relates an incident regarding the woman servant of Rabbi Judah the Prince who was known for her learning. When Rabbi Judah was ill, she ascended the roof and prayed the following: "The immortals desire Rabbi [to join them] and the mortals desire Rabbi [to join them]. May it be His will that the mortals may overpower the immortals." However, when she observed that his illness was incurable, noting how often he entered the privy, painfully removing his *tefillin* and putting them on again, she prayed, "May it be His will that the immortals have power over the mortals." As his colleagues incessantly continued their prayers for God's mercy, the servant picked up a jar and threw it down from the roof to the ground. For a moment they ceased praying and the soul of Rabbi Judah departed to its eternal rest (Ketubot 104a).

Elsewhere the famous Talmudic commentator, the Ran, cites the above incident and concludes that one should pray for God's compassion to take the life of a suffering patient who is incurably ill with no chance of recovery. The view of the Ran is not accepted by all authorities, however. Eliezer Waldenberg, a contemporary Israeli scholar, does not permit a prayer for the death of an incurable patient. He says that those who permit the prayer do so only for strangers and not for relatives of the patient since their motive may be impure, such as the unconscious desire to be rid of their responsibility to the patient.

It is understood that the decision over life and death must be left to God and that one may not hasten the death of another person by his own hands. The Mishna explicitly states that unless we are certain that the patient has died, we cannot close his eyes or fold his hands, the normal procedure after death. Although the patient may be dying, if by touching him we hasten his death by an instant, we are responsible for taking his life. The Talmud compares life to a candle. If we touch the candle, we may cause the flame to be extinguished. Even if it were already flickering, our touch alone could extinguish the flame. Similarly, by merely touching the dying patient, we can hasten his death even by a brief moment. The conclusion may be refuted by modern science but it does serve to illustrate the rabbinic emphasis on preserving the life of another person until the very end.

64 Jews are expected to accept tragedy without complaint

Occasionally we meet a person whose intense religious faith helps him accept personal tragedy without expressing anger or complaint. We tend to admire such spiritual strength in the face of adversity, but not every religious person is able to endure the loss of a family member or friend without asking why.

When Jacob was told that his son Joseph was dead, the Torah comments that "he refused to be comforted." When King David learned of his son's death he expressed the natural parental anguish: "O my son Absalom, my son, my son Absalom. Would I have died for thee, O Absalom, my son, my son." The prophet Jeremiah envisioned the matriarch Rachel weeping bitterly for her children. Rachel "refused to be comforted."

One of the profound themes in the Book of Job deals with God's reaction to Job's contention that justice is absent in God's world. Job's friends who came to comfort him after all his afflictions insist that Job had no right to complain. He was a sinner being repaid for his wrongdoing. He could be reconciled by accepting and submitting to God's chastisement without questioning God's justice, they declared.

In the last chapter of the book Job is finally reconciled with God by accepting the mystery and harmony of the universe which he admits is beyond human understanding. Accepting the sublime beauty of God's world soothes his pain and provides a renewed faith in God's justice.

At this juncture the reader would expect God to praise the friends for having asked Job to submit to God without complaint. Not so. God tells Eliphaz that he and his friends, and not Job, have incensed God. "My anger is kindled against you and your two friends, for you have not spoken the truth about Me as has My servant Job." They will be forgiven only if Job pleads for them.

During the brief period from the death of a relative until the funeral, the mourner is known as an *onain*. He is exempted from the performance of the commandments such as reciting the *shema* or recitation of the daily prayers. Rabbi Joseph Soloveitchik analyzes the reason for this legal exemption. The *onain* during this initial stage of mourning dehumanizes himself. He feels that man is not human, that he is no different than the beast. He tells himself that if death is the destiny of all men, why then pretend that we are the choicest of all creatures? Why be moral?

Soloveitchik contends that Jewish law shows great compassion for these torturing thoughts and doubts. It does not command the mourner to deny them. "It permitted the mourner to have his way for a while and has ruled that the latter be relieved of all *mitzvot*," according to Soloveitchik. Only after the burial does Jewish law require the mourner to "pick up the debris of his own shattered personality." By reciting the *kaddish* at the grave, the mourner enters the second stage, in which his despair gives way to intelligent sadness and his self-negation is transformed to self-affirmation. Only then is he ready to become part of the community once again and to be uplifted by the religious requirements of his faith.

It is apparent then that Judaism does not regard bouts with skepticism after tragedy as heresy. It is natural for a mourner to question basic religious assumptions. The entire mourning period with its detailed requirements for eleven months is intended to restore the mourner's faith in God and His creation.

65 The Mourner's *kaddish* is a prayer for the dead

The belief that the Mourner's *kaddish* is a prayer on behalf of the departed stems from the tradition of reciting this prayer for eleven months after the death of a parent. It would appear then that the *kaddish* is a prayer for the dead—a common misconception.

There is no word or phrase in the *kaddish* referring to death. Nowhere in this prayer is there even a hint that the worshipper asks God's special protection for the deceased; there is no reference to the world-to-come or the immortality of the soul. And most significant, no mention is provided for the name of the departed such as is found in the Memorial Prayer (*el maleh rahamim*). Only in the Burial *kaddish* recited at the cemetery do we find a specific reference to death.

Why then is the mourner required to recite the *kaddish* prayer for eleven months, and every year on the anniversary date of death? The recitation of *kaddish* by the mourner developed at a relatively late date, probably in the Middle Ages. We cannot determine exactly how this association developed, but it has been suggested that the son would take an active part in the Torah discussion at the House of Study after his father's death to honor his memory. After the discussion he was privileged to recite the closing Scholar's *kaddish*.

In the course of time this custom of studying Torah in honor of the deceased was practiced with less regularity and only the *kaddish* was retained as a mark of respect for the deceased. A shortened form of the Scholar's *kaddish* recited by the son, came to be known as the Mourner's *kaddish*, though no mention of death is to be found in it.

What then *does* the *kaddish* convey? It is an affirmation of hope that the Kingship of God may be accepted by all mankind. By implication the *kaddish* expresses a resolve by the worshipper to sanctify God's name by practicing the divine attributes of justice and compassion in his own personal life.

For the mourner the recitation of the *kaddish* also represents an emphasis on life and the living even in the midst of personal anguish. It helps the mourner to elevate his preoccupation with his own tragedy into hope for a better life for all people. A morbid mood of grieving over the dead is transformed into a more confident and optimistic attitude. Another compelling reason for reciting the *kaddish* is that it brings the mourner into the synagogue in the presence of other mourners and worshippers. There he may find emotional support and sympathy during his period of bereavement.

66 Only sons may recite
the Mourner's *kaddish*

It is true that Jewish law requires only sons of the deceased to recite the Mourner's *kaddish*. Where there are no sons, daughters are not required to say *kaddish*. The Orthodox practice is to suggest that the daughter honor her deceased parents by responding "Amen" as others recite the *kaddish*. Doing so, she is regarded as though she had personally recited the *kaddish*.

Some Orthodox rabbis, however, have not discouraged a daughter from reciting the *kaddish*. An orthodox rabbi, Hayim Halevi Donin in his guide, *To Be a Jew*, writes that "she may rise to recite *kaddish* at religious services if she feels inclined to do so. Some religious scholars do not share this latter view."

In Conservative and Reform congregations women are encouraged to stand with the male mourners and recite the *kaddish*. Conservative Jews are guided by the view of its Committee on Jewish Laws and Standards, which formulated the opinion (1974) that "the obligation to recite *kaddish* for a deceased relative may be fulfilled by women who shall be encouraged to say *kaddish* especially when there are no males obligated." Today it is widely accepted that a daughter may recite the *kaddish*, especially on the Sabbath, even if there are sons who are also reciting it.

Not only sons or daughters of the deceased may recite *kaddish*. Judaism regards any individual, even a non-relative of the deceased, who has undertaken to recite *kaddish* for a friend as performing a special meritorious act.

Although Jewish law permits a non-relative to recite the *kaddish* if the deceased left no children or if his children cannot attend daily service, the practice of "hiring" someone for this purpose should be discouraged. The custom lends itself to commercialization and degrades a hallowed tradition. In many cases, mourners have treated the requirement to recite the *kaddish* lightly, taking advantage of the "dispensation" even when attending the daily service posed no difficulty for them.

67 Mourners sit on boxes to avoid comfort during *shiva*

The tradition of sitting on boxes during the period of *shiva* is not to make the mourner feel uncomfortable and certainly not to have him suffer more than necessary. There is no rule that requires mourners to sit on boxes. What is required of them is that they not sit on chairs of normal height. The simple removal of a pillow from the living room chair or sofa fulfills the traditional requirement. Upholstered chairs may also be used, provided they are lower than ordinary chairs.

In ancient times it was customary to sit on inverted beds, and when this custom was discontinued mourners would sit on the floor. The use of boxes or stools provided by many funeral parlors is widely used but not because these are specified by the Jewish tradition.

Different reasons have been offered to explain why mourners are required to sit in a lower position than usual. One explanation is that mourners are expected to sit closer to the earth in which the deceased relative is buried, a symbolic gesture of feeling spiritually united with a loved one in spite of physical separation.

Contrary to popular belief, then, the Jewish tradition does not request that the mourner experience added discomfort to intensify the normal grief that comes with losing a member of the family. As far back

as biblical times the Israelites were warned against inflicting self-punishment in imitation of their pagan
neighbors, who tortured their bodies to express their
grief in mourning.

68 Mourners are required to dress in black

If one were searching Jewish sources for the basis of wearing black mourning clothes, it would not be difficult to find support in the Talmudic tradition. The *aggadah* (rabbinic lore) quotes Moses as saying: "Joshua, put on black clothes after my death." When Simon the Just (fourth cent. B.C.E.) foretold his coming death, he was asked how he knew. He answered: "Every day of atonement an old man, dressed in white would accompany me as I entered the Holy of Holies. But today I was accompanied by an old man dressed in black."

Israel Abrahams, author of *Jewish Life in the Middle Ages*, writes that wearing black clothing was widespread among the Jews in many countries including Spain, Germany and Italy. Since they were "Mourners of Zion," the Jews wore the color most associated with grief, modesty, and "its applicability to their persecuted state." In Medieval Europe, then, many Jews wore black even when not in mourning. Black best expressed the somber mood of a downtrodden people.

In England until the second half of the nineteenth century the family of the deceased was provided with mourners' cloaks which were worn during the seven-day *shiva* period. Nevertheless there is no law requiring Jews to wear black clothing at the funeral or during the week of mourning. Even the wearing of dark clothes is not required of mourners, although it seems appropriate to be clothed in subdued colors.

69 Clothes belonging to the deceased must be discarded

Many personal beliefs regarding the clothing of the deceased have been passed down from one generation to the other. Some people have been told that the clothes should remain in place and not be disturbed. This belief is probably based on the irrational hope that one's beloved relative will physically return to life at some future time. Those survivors who find it especially difficult to accept the reality of death will often insist on keeping the clothes of the deceased in the closet for an indefinite period.

Others assume that clothing belonging to the deceased must be discarded. This belief is based on the superstition that some misfortune will befall one who wears clothing once worn by the deceased. There is also the fear of mistaken identity; the living could be called by the name of the dead person if he wears his clothes in public.

There is no religious reason why clothes of the deceased should be discarded. A relative or friend should have no hesitation in wearing them. Or they may be given to a charity that helps to clothe the poor. We should encourage the charitable gift because it may help to prolong the life of a needy person.

To discard clothing that may still be worn is expressly prohibited by Jewish tradition. To discard any useful object such as food or clothing violates *bal tashhit*, a prohibition against needless waste or destruction. The underlying thought is that ultimately we do not really own anything. Everything man possesses rightfully belongs to God—even our food or clothing. All possessions have been loaned on condition that we make wise use of them. The implication is that we should also be prepared to give these objects over to others when we no longer have personal use for them.

The traditional explanation for the wearing of the shroud by the deceased is that it discourages ostentation. The simplest clothing is worn by rich and poor alike. There may be another, more subtle reason why the more observant Jews are not buried in a suit or dress: These can still be worn by a living person whereas the shroud, which is worn at death, has no practical value for the living.

70 Jewish law requires children whose parents are alive to leave the service during *yizkor*

It is a custom, not a law, for children whose parents are alive to leave the synagogue when the *Yizkor* Memorial Service is recited four times during the year. Among the Sefardic Jews everyone remains in the service during *yizkor*.

The Israeli scholar Eliyahu Kitov in his book *Sefer Hatodah*, presents some of the original reasons why children whose parents were alive followed the custom of leaving the service: If they were to remain in the synagogue, they could arouse the jealousy of those children whose parents had died; if children with parents were to remain, they might recite the *yizkor* through error, thereby tempting fate; by remaining in the Synagogue yet keeping silent while others were reciting their prayers, these children would find themselves in an awkward situation. It is apparent that some of these reasons have no rational basis, yet the custom continues to be widely observed in many traditional synagogues.

Many synagogues today encourage all children to remain during *yizkor* so as not to interrupt the decorum of the religious service. Children who are fortunate to have their parents are advised to recite a memorial prayer for their grandparents, other relatives or a friend who has died. Some prayerbooks include a *yizkor* prayer on behalf of the martyrs of Israel who died for the sanctification of God's name — an appropriate prayer for anyone in the congregation.

We cannot judge the validity of an ancient Jewish custom for ourselves merely by examining its origin. Rather than relying on the origin of a custom, we should determine whether its meaning can be interpreted to contain a redeeming social or moral value. Unlike many ancient customs which tend to strengthen Jewish belief and commitment, such as the recitation of yizkor, the archaic custom of requesting children to leave the service during the yizkor discourages them from confronting the reality of death and sharing the loss of grandparents and other relatives with their parents.

71 Judaism is concerned only with this life, not with what happens after we die

It is true that Jewish theology is less concerned with life after death than are other ancient religions. For example, the ancient Egyptians were more involved with death than with life and would fill their tombs with precious stones and provisions for the afterlife of the departed. The ancient Hebrews totally rejected this otherworldly emphasis. Although Christian theology was greatly influenced by biblical and rabbinic Judaism, it also became preoccupied with life after death and taught its adherents to value the afterlife as more precious than one's earthly existence.

To deny Judaism's concern with what happens after death is a distortion of Jewish theology. It is true that the Torah does not refer to life beyond the grave, but merely to *sheol*, a nebulous home of the departed. Only in Daniel, one of the later books of the Bible, is there a specific reference to resurrection: "Many of those that sleep in the dust of the earth will awake, some to eternal life, others to reproaches, to everlasting abhorrence" (12:2).

Only after the biblical period, during the reign of the Maccabees, did a deeper concern for the afterlife became important to the Jewish community. During the

Maccabean period when many righteous men were dying to defend the principles of Judaism, people were told that there was a life beyond the present that justified martyrdom in the battle against the godless foe.

During the rabbinic period the two concepts of immortality of the soul and resurrection became clearly adopted as basic Jewish beliefs. The Pharisees, in contrast to the Sadducees, accepted both doctrines. Throughout the Talmudic literature we find various sages expressing how they envision the hereafter. It was generally agreed that the deceased do not experience physical sensation, only a spiritual existence. Rav expressed the widely accepted view:

> In the world to come there is no eating nor drinking nor propagation nor business nor jealousy nor hatred nor competition, but the righteous sit with crowns on their heads enjoying the radiance of the Divine Presence (Berakhot 17a).

The Medieval philosophers were divided in their opinions regarding resurrection. Saadia Gaon held the view that when the body is resurrected it will then endure to eternity. Maimonides also believed in resurrection as a basic principle of Judaism, but, unlike Saadia, he contended that the body would exist only for another lifetime, not forever. Maimonides with his scientific mind could not conceive of the body living on indefinitely without death and decay. Only the soul would live forever in the world to come.

Although Jewish theology is concerned with life after death, the hereafter remains a mystery, open to individual speculation and interpretation. The Jew is not required to accept one definitive view of the afterlife as a test of loyalty to his faith. The Jewish view is best expressed in this enigmatic statement found in *Ethics of the*

Fathers: "Better is one hour of repentance and good works in this world than all the life of the world to come; yet one hour of bliss in the world to come is more exquisite than all of life in this world." No sensation of happiness in this life can be compared to the afterlife, but the highest good that man can actively choose is to live a moral life here in this world.

72 Reincarnation is totally alien to Jewish thought

The doctrine of reincarnation or transmigration of souls is not totally alien to Judaism although it is not referred to in the Talmud nor is it mentioned by such prominent Jewish philosophers as Judah Halevi and Maimonides.

Not until the twelfth century, when *Sefer Ha-Bahir* was written, does the doctrine of reincarnation appear in Jewish literature. Known in Hebrew as *gilgul*, reincarnation is later discussed in detail by the mystic Nahmanides and especially in the *Zohar*, the basic text of Jewish mysticism.

This belief in *gilgul* was introduced by Jewish mystics in an attempt to explain the age-old question of why the righteous suffer and the wicked prosper. They believed that if a righteous person suffered, the new person who received the soul of the righteous one would have a happy and joyful life. On the other hand, a sinful person's soul entering the body of another would endure a life of suffering. In time, the belief in reincarnation included the soul's migrating into animals or plants as punishment for the sins of the wicked.

The doctrine appears to be strikingly similar in many respects to the Hindu belief in reincarnation. We cannot be certain that the Jewish doctrine is directly derived from Hinduism. Some scholars believe that the

Jewish mystics became familiar with reincarnation through the Arabs who converted many Hindus to Islam. Even after their conversion to Islam, many Hindus stubbornly continued to maintain some of their old traditions, such as the belief in reincarnation. The Jews who came into close cultural contact with the Muslims during the Golden Age in Spain may have learned about reincarnation from Muslims and incorporated this belief into their mystical tradition.

Another theory is associated with the extensive travels of Spanish Jews to the Far East. As merchants of international trade, Spanish Jews came into direct contact with the Hindus in India, returning not only with merchandise but with religious doctrines which attracted the attention of Jewish mystics in Spain.

The vast majority of contemporary Jews do not accept reincarnation as basic to their faith, yet we cannot simply dismiss the role of certain mystical beliefs in the evolution of Jewish religious thought.

SOME
COMMON HEBREW
EXPRESSIONS
Their Uncommon
Meanings

73 A *mitzvah* is a good deed

Many people speak of a *mitzvah* as referring to any simple act that brings pleasure to another person. For example, a parent may request a child to "Do a *mitzvah* today and visit your grandparents." True, any act of kindness or compassion may be loosely defined as a *mitzvah*, but *mitzvah* conveys much more than a good turn for the day.

A *mitzvah* is not simply a voluntary act but a religious commandment, implying *One Who Commands*, namely, God. Rabbi Nahman of Bratzlav, the *hasidic* sage, further refined its meaning when he said, "Every act done in agreement with God's will is a *mitzvah*."

In the Torah the term *mitzvah* carries a general rather than specific meaning. It embraces all of God's requirements of the Israelites found in the Five Books of Moses — statutes, ordinances, testimonies and observances.

In the Talmudic era all the individual biblical precepts and prohibitions were placed in categories. Rabbi Simlai, a Palestinian scholar, speaks of 613 commandments that were revealed to Moses at Mt. Sinai. "365 prohibitions are equal in number to the solar days and 248 positive commandments correspond to the number of limbs of the human body." These *mitzvot* range from the commandments required only of the High Priest in the Temple to a simple act of kindness required of every Jew.

The *mitzvot* are further divided into two categories: "The commandments between man and God," which may be translated loosely as ritual, and "commandments between man and his fellow," which are usually understood as ethical requirements.

Although the commandments are not equal in importance—some are "light" and some "weighty"—the rabbis cautioned people not to decide for themselves which to observe and which to ignore, since the true reward for fulfilling each precept is not known to mortals, only to God. And speaking of reward, a person should not anticipate any material recompense for observing a *mitzvah* other than the satisfaction of knowing that "one *mitzvah* generates another and one *averah* (transgression) generates another." Observing a *mitzvah*, then, carries a cumulative spiritual reward.

The traditional Jew looks upon a *mitzvah* almost as if it were a familiar object rather than a concept. He speaks of "acquiring *mitzvot*," "adorning himself with mitzvot before God." Jewish tradition has allegorically compared mitzvot to a friend, one's offspring, and to one's garments—all regarded as basic necessities of life.

74 Bar mitzvah is a ceremony that takes place in the synagogue

Although most Jews associate *bar mitzvah* with a special synagogue ceremony at age thirteen, this is not the technical meaning of the term. A male Jewish child automatically becomes *bar mitzvah* upon attaining his thirteenth birthday, whether he and the family celebrate the special occasion or not. He becomes obligated for the first time to observe all the commandments that are required of an adult Jew—thus the term bar mitzvah, which literally means "a son of the commandment." Freely translated, the term means "one who is obligated to observe the commandments." In essence he remains a bar mitzvah for the rest of his life, not merely for the one day when he is called to the Torah or participates in the Service.

Some of the *mitzvot* that the *bar mitzvah* assumes for the first time are being called to the Torah, being counted in a *minyan* (quorum of ten), wearing *tefillin* (phylacteries), and fasting on Yom Kippur. Until the son has reached the age of thirteen, the father is responsible for his deeds or misdeeds; now that the son is a full member of the Jewish community, the religious responsibilities are entirely his to observe.

Why was the thirteenth year established as the turning point in the child's life? Jewish law recognized this age as the beginning of physical maturity and a stage in which young people could exercise control over their desires and emotions. In Midrashic literature the age of thirteen was the turning point in the life of Abraham when he rejected the idol worship of his father, Terah. At thirteen Jacob separated from his brother Esau to pursue the study of Torah. In more recent history this was the age of transition when the young man completed his elementary edu-cation to pursue advanced studies in the *Bet Hamidrash* (academy of higher learning).

A Jewish girl traditionally attained her religious and legal maturity at age twelve, corresponding to her more advanced physical maturity. She becomes a *bat mitzvah* for the rest of her life, and she too is required to assume the responsibilities of Jewish adulthood. Whether she participates in a special religious service or not, her status as "daughter of the commandment" is automatically conferred upon her.

75   The meaning of Torah is law

There is no specific word in biblical Hebrew for law. There are words to express a statute, a ruling, a commandment, but not law.

Torah is frequently translated as "the law," and the subtle error is understandable. Much of the material in the second half of Exodus and in the Books of Leviticus, Numbers, and Deuteronomy deals with regulations required of the Israelites. The term *law*, however, is of Greek origin, and not Hebrew, deriving from the word *nomos* meaning "law." In the Greek translation of the Bible adopted by the Christian Church, the Torah's last book is called *Deutero-nomos* (in English, *Deuteronomy*) meaning the "second law," because this book reviews the many laws found in the previous Books of the Torah.

What then does Torah mean? It is derived from the verb meaning "to teach" or "to guide." More specifically the term Torah refers to instruction or guidance rather than law.

Torah is more than a word. It defies any attempt at exact translation and can only be understood on many levels:

— In its most literal sense, Torah is the sacred scroll containing the Five Books of Moses or the Pentateuch.

— In its wider meaning the term also refers to the *content* of the scroll, and in addition, all the sacred books which are included in the Holy Scriptures. These later books, such as Isaiah, the Song of Songs, the Psalms, while not literally Torah, are called Torah because they reflect the spirit of the Five Books of Moses.

Torah may also include the vast literature of the rabbis known as the Talmud, developed from about the third century before the Common Era to the fifth century of the Common Era.

—The commentaries on the Bible and the Talmud written by the ancient philosophers and moralists down to the present era come under a still wider definition of Torah.

—Torah is also used synonymously with Jewish education. Whether studying the Jewish sources on one's own or in a formal classroom, the student is engaging in Torah.

In sum, Torah has come to include the Jewish literary heritage, the entire creative output of the Jewish people from Sinai to the present day. To restrict the meaning of Torah exclusively to the law leads to a misunderstanding of what the concept has come to mean to the Jewish people.

76 The meaning of *tzedakah* is charity

When Jews use the term *tzedakah*, they usually understand it as charity, but this is an inadequate translation. Charity is derived from the French *charite*, originating from the Latin *caritaten*, meaning love or kindness. *Tzedakah* derives from the Hebrew *tzedek*, meaning an act of justice or righteousness. *Tzedakah* does include an attitude of love and kindness, but it involves more than an emotion. It is an act that a person is required to perform because it is prescribed by Jewish law. *Tzedakah* is not an abstraction. It exists only when it becomes a tangible act, when the heart directs the hand.

The sages had only harsh words for the person who wishes to exempt himself from *tzedakah*. "Whosoever conceals his eyes from *tzedakah*, it is as though he were worshipping idols" (Ketubot, 68a). "Whoever has the opportunity to perform an act of *tzedakah* and refuses, to save a person and refuses, causes himself to die" (*Tana d'bei Eliyahu Zuta*, 1). Frequently the rabbis would use strong or even shocking expressions in order to teach more effectively the importance of values such as *tzedakah*. Their intention was clear: To neglect the suffering of others weakens a person's character causing a loss of his humanity.

Tzedakah is not confined to giving money outright to those in need. It also includes other acts of benevolence. Maimonides regards the highest form of *tzedakah* to be when one "assists a poor Jew by providing him with a gift or a loan or by making him a partner or finding him employment in order to strengthen him to such a degree that he no longer has to request aid from others."

Maimonides also lists other non-monetary forms of *tzedakah* to fulfill a person's needs in accordance with what he lacks:

> If he has no wife, you are required to make provisions for his marriage; if the poor person is a woman you are required to provide for her marriage. Even if a poor person, who was once rich, was accustomed to ride about on a horse with a servant running before him, you are required to purchase a horse and servant to run before him, for it is said (Deut. 15:8), "Sufficient for his needs in that which he lacks" (*Mishneh Torah*, "*Matnot Aniyim*," 7:3).

If necessary, soothing words constitute an act of *tzedakah*.

> If a poor person requests help and you having nothing in your possession to give him, calm him with words; it is forbidden to be angry at him or to shout at him, for his heart is broken and crushed (*Mishneh Torah*, "*Matnot Aniyim*," 10:5).

Because *tzedakah* is not voluntary but a mandatory act of justice, legal means were established in medieval times to require residents of a community to contribute. The longer a person remains in the town, the greater his responsibility to share in the needs of the community.

A person living in a community thirty days may be coerced to contribute to the *kupah* (fund) together with other members of the community. If he lives there for three months he may be coerced to give to the *tamhui* (soup kitchen). If he resides there six months he may be coerced to perform *tzedakah* for the purpose of clothing the city's poor. If he lives there nine months he may be coerced to perform *tzedakah* to maintain the cemeteries in which the poor are buried, in addition to all other matters pertaining to burial (*Mishneh Torah*, "*Matnot Aniyim*," 9:12).

77 *Kosher* refers only to permitted foods

It is true that the term *kosher* (or *kasher*) most often refers to foods that are permitted to be eaten, in contrast to non-*kosher* or *terefah*. But *kosher* is also used to denote objects that are fit for ritual use. Following are the most common uses of the word when it does not refer to food.

The word *kasher* where it is found in the Book of Esther conveys the idea of right or proper ("... and the thing seems right before the king"). The same meaning was given in later Rabbinic literature to objects that are ritually fit for use.

A Torah Scroll that is fit to be read is called *kosher* in contrast to a Torah Scroll that is in need of repair because letters may be faded or the parchment torn. Such a "non-*kosher*" scroll is called *pasul*, unfit for public reading.

Likewise, only *tefillin* (phylacteries) that are maintained in good condition may be worn in prayer. If the parchment inside the black capsules has been removed, then the *tefillin* are no longer *kosher* until the missing sections are replaced.

The biblical passages in the *mezuzah*, which is affixed to the doorpost, must be written on parchment and not on paper. Otherwise it is not *kosher*, acceptable for use on the doorpost. Every *tallit*, (prayer shawl) must contain a required number of fringes to be regarded as *kosher*. A *mikveh*, ritualarium, must be constructed according to specifications to qualify as *kosher*.

Even people are termed *kosher* under certain circumstances. For example, only competent witnesses are *kosher* and may testify in accordance with Jewish law.

In recent years, the term *kosher* has taken on popular usage in English speaking countries to convey the following meanings: Authentic, legal or O.K.

OPINIONS ABOUT JEWS
Some Common Fallacies

78 Historically Jews resented being restricted to the ghetto

The word *ghetto* is probably derived from the Italian *geto* meaning iron-foundry. It was near the iron-foundry in Venice where there was established the first technical ghetto in which all Jews were forced to live and Gentiles were excluded. Although restrictive ghettos existed in Sicily and Germany centuries before the Venetian ghetto was erected in 1516, the laws were not strictly enforced against those who chose to live outside the Jewish area.

Although the coercive ghettos were humiliating—they were usually congested and located in the poorest section of the town—the closed Jewish quarter was not resented by those Jews who were forced to live in them. Contrary to popular belief, the medieval ghettos were often welcomed by members of the Jewish community because they felt more secure among their own people. Within the ghetto they were able to develop their institutions and to fulfill their social, cultural and religious needs without intimidation from the general population.

Jacob Katz writes in his book *Exclusiveness and Tolerance*:

> The Jew whose work took him out of the ghetto and among the Gentiles for the day or the week felt as if

he were leaving his natural environment and entering a strange world. Only on returning home in the evening, or at least for the Sabbath, did he find any satisfaction beyond the goal of earning a living.

Ghetto life also provided the medieval Jewish community with greater physical security. Two official gatekeepers appointed by the town would close the gates from sunset to sunrise. Although the locked gates were sometimes helpful in preventing attacks from the outside, fanatics intent on attacking Jews were not deterred by walls or locked gates. The ghetto did not always provide the physical security that Jews hoped for.

Generally, the Jews did not protest against the restrictive laws separating them from their Gentile neighbors. The distinguished historian Salo Baron found evidence that in Verona and Mantua (Italy) the erection of the ghetto walls was even celebrated by the local community with an annual festival modeled after Purim.

Unlike the ghetto, laws requiring the wearing of the Jewish badge were deeply resented by the Jewish community. They regarded the badge as a visible sign of degradation. Because they were so easily identified, every Jew was a potential target of attack. In addition, his business activity was severely restricted. Wherever possible, Jews used their influence to seek the revocation of laws requiring them to wear the Jewish badge or any other article of clothing that made them vulnerable to derision and abuse.

79 Jews were never fighters until the Warsaw Ghetto uprising against the Nazis

Jews have often been accused of failing to defend themselves, instead passively accepting a fate dealt to them by their enemies. Anti-Semites have described them as weaklings and cowards; some Jews as well have criticized their own people for lack of courage in years past in contrast to the brave spirit of the Israelis. One reason that many of the early Jewish pioneers in Palestine glorified the biblical era and not the centuries of exile in Europe was precisely because the former provided them with courageous heroes after whom they could model their lives; they could not identify with those European Jews who refused to resist their enemies.

It is true that, with a few notable exceptions, from the time of the Jewish rebellion against Rome in the second century until the beginning of the twentieth century Jews did not organize to defend themselves against their enemies. Yet their failure to strike back could not be attributed to a belief in pacificism. Neither the Bible nor the Talmud encouraged non-resistance.

The Jewish communities in Europe, often impoverished and scattered, were not strong enough to mount an effective opposition against a large group of armed peasants or an army of crusaders who were passionate enemies of the Jews. The Jews, lacking the arms and physical security to defend themselves, often relied on a nobleman and his army to give them protection, naturally for a price.

It was not until the Russian pogroms erupted in 1881-82 that Jews began to organize self-defense groups. Equipped with light arms, the Jewish defenders relied on their numerical strength to try to prevent the mobs from entering their neighborhoods.

The pogroms in 1903, especially one in Kishinev, created a renewed interest in self-defense. The more militant mood among young Jews was largely a response to the poet Bialik's "City of Slaughter," in which he sharply criticized the shame of acquiescence of the "calves for the slaughter." However, despite their valiant efforts, Jews were attacked by the Russian army with the blessings of the Czarist government. Many Jews fell defending themselves; others were captured and brought to trial.

In 1905 organized defense groups existed in forty-two cities. The nucleus of their movement came from the Jewish labor parties and their military units with a following from the Jewish masses. In that year 132 fighters died in self-defense. After the revolution in Russia there were renewed attempts to organize Jewish self-defense groups to repel bands of attackers such as the dreaded Cossacks. Despite their valiant efforts, however, the Jewish defenders and their leaders died in battle.

Although their organized efforts usually ended in defeat, the attempt was not futile. Out of the Jews' experience in self-defense in Eastern Europe eventually came the *Haganah*, the defense force that played such an essential role in successfully defending the Jewish community of Palestine against the Arabs before the State was declared in 1948.

80 Jews have shown
a genius for business

Over the years some Jewish adversaries, as well as Jews themselves, have claimed that the Jewish people have an innate talent for business; it has been said that business acumen is imbedded in their national character.

Werner Sombart, a German political economist (d. 1941), theorized that the Jews were responsible for the establishment and growth of capitalism in Europe. He contended that since the Jews were refused admission to the guilds which controlled commerce in the medieval cities, they broke away from the restrictions imposed on them in the city and became pioneers in international trade, thus founding the capitalist system. Sombart maintained that the Jewish mind — "concrete, stubborn and systematic" — was ideally suited to the creation of a capitalist economy.

There is little question that the Jews played a significant role in the development of capitalism, but Sombart's general thesis has been widely criticized by other scholars. In addition, the Nazis exploited Sombart's views to support their vicious propaganda against the Jews.

The claim that Jews have historically shown a talent for business *can* be easily supported. They have enjoyed a long experience in commerce, especially since the early Middle Ages, when they were forbidden by the Church to own property or to enter the guilds. The Jews were forced into lending money in order to survive economically. Since the Church prohibited Christians from moneylending, regarding it as sinful, the Jews entered the field; Jewish law did not forbid the charging of interest for business loans so long as the rates were not excessive. (Exacting interest from individuals in need is forbidden by biblical and Talmudic law.)

Eventually the Church relaxed its own prohibition against moneylending, and Jews were forced out of this profitable area. They found other ways to remain active in commerce, such as in the diamond trade. Diamonds were frequently used as collateral for loans, and Jews also could carry diamonds with them if they were forced to leave their community in haste. For many years Jews were predominant in the diamond trade in Portugal; they traded extensively with India, which was the main source of uncut diamonds. When they were driven from Portugal, they moved to Holland, which became the new center of the diamond trade.

William Helmreich, a prominent sociologist, suggests that the Jewish religion's emphasis on abstract thinking may also account for the Jew's skill in business affairs. The study of the Talmud in particular with its concentration on abstract ideas helped to sharpen the mind of the Jew and enable him to transfer his intellectual interest to the field of economics.

Thus when capitalism became important to the modern world, Jews were in a position to benefit from it. After all, interest, futures, options, stocks and, most importantly money itself were abstractions ... It was not so much a question of superior skills as having the skills that modern society most needed.

To claim that the Jews possess an innate talent or genius for making money is as far-fetched as the theory that they possess a genius for music or science even though many have excelled in these fields. These attempts to stereotype the Jews cannot be verified. With the many areas that are open to young Jews in America, many have chosen occupations and professions that are unrelated to the business world. The distorted image of the Jew as an inherently astute or shrewd businessman may become extinct in the course of time unless the anti-Semite persists in exploiting the myth.

81 A true Zionist believes that all Jews must be prepared to settle in Israel

At the turn of the century Solomon Schechter, head of the Jewish Theological Seminary, delivered an important statement on Zionism. Schechter asserted that Zionism could not be adequately defined. For some Jews Zionism represented the rebirth of the Jewish consciousness; for the pious Zionism meant religious revival; for those who wanted to preserve the cultural aspects of Judaism Zionism was a "path leading to the goal of Jewish culture"; to a fourth group it meant the "last and only solution to the Jewish problems."

Schechter observed that on one point all Zionists were in agreement: It is not only desirable, but essential that Palestine be recovered for the purpose of forming a home where at least a portion of Jews would be able to lead an independent national life. Although his statement on Zionism was first published in 1906 it may still serve, with minor changes in wording, as a working definition of what it means to be a Zionist.

Not everyone accepted Schechter's view of Zionism. Some Zionist thinkers and activists took a dim view of Jewish life in the Diaspora. Theodor Herzl and Max Nordau both felt that in time all committed Jews would return to their historic homeland and the remaining small minority, consisting of the wealthy and assimilated, would soon disappear.

The first Prime Minister of the founding State of Israel, David Ben-Gurion, also expressed this view. He made a distinction between "friends of Israel," those who supported the State, and true Zionists. The term "Zionists," Ben-Gurion felt, could properly be applied only to those who were preparing themselves and their families, no matter how comfortable their present home, to come eventually as immigrants to the new Jewish State. After much debate, in 1968 Ben -Gurion's opinion was accepted as Israel's official view. In a proclamation issued by the Jerusalem program of the Zionist congress, the concept of aliyah, personal migration, was accepted as the ultimate ideal and a requirement of belonging to any legitimate Zionist group.

Many contemporary Jews who have not accepted the call for personal *aliyah* nevertheless regard themselves as staunch Zionists. They are painfully aware of the problems of Jewish illiteracy and the growing problems of assimilation outside of Israel. They encourage the concept of *aliyah* for those who wish to settle in Israel, and yet they are not prepared to uproot themselves and their families. They know that anti-Semitism continues to exist in the Western countries, but they contend that it will not interfere with their future as individuals nor with the status of the Jewish community in which they live.

The sharp debate that took place in the sixties regarding whether Zionists are required to prepare for *aliyah* has been muted in recent years. There is a growing awareness among Israelis and even among those who have chosen *aliyah* for themselves that a significant number of Jews will continue to live outside of Israel.

To denigrate them for failing to migrate to Israel or to question whether they are genuine Zionists will not alter their plans.

In 1955 Mordecai M. Kaplan already saw the need to rethink the meaning of Zionism. In *A New Zionism*, he wrote:

Zionism has to be redefined, so as to assure a place for Diaspora Judaism. Such a redefinition, while affirming the indispensability of *Eretz Yisrael* ("the Land of Israel") as the home of Judaism for Jews throughout the world, would have to stress the peoplehood, or the oneness and indivisibility of world Jewry.

82 Israel should not be called a Jewish State just as the United States is not called a Christian country

Most Jews take exception to the often expressed view that the United States is a Christian society, even though the vast majority of Americans are Christians. Christmas is celebrated as a national holiday in the United States and the holiday spirit pervades everywhere for weeks before. Although most Jews are affected by the predominance of Christian influences throughout the year, they still maintain that America must not be identified as a Christian society; to do so would contravene the First Amendment of the Bill of Rights in the United States Constitution: "Congress should make no law respecting an establishment of religion. ..."

By the same token, some Jews are hesitant to call Israel a Jewish State for the very reason that America should not be referred to as a Christian country. Since Israel is also a democracy, they reason that it should not be associated with a particular religious preference.

But the words Christian and Jewish are not really opposites. The former always bears a religious connotation; the latter carries a broader meaning and is not confined to a religion. It includes as well the cultural life of the Jewish people, and even the creative achievements of the secular Jewish community in Israel.

Therefore, when referring to the Jewish State we do not imply that Israel is or should become a theocracy, even though a small but vocal minority conceive it as such. Israel is a Jewish State in the sense that it is dedicated to the preservation and promotion of Jewish values and Jewish cultural creativity. For example, Hebrew has been revived as a living language in the State of Israel. Most Israelis are called by their Hebrew names, and many family names have been recast into the Hebrew. Streets are named after great Jewish personalities and significant events in Jewish history.

But most significant, Israel has become a homeland for all Jews who wish to reside there; automatic citizenship is conferred on any Jew who makes *aliyah* from any part of the world. This "Law of Return" would not have been possible if Israel did not regard itself as Jewish State.

It is a moot question whether Israel would continue to be called a Jewish State if Jews were no longer the majority. This possibility has become a major concern in recent years and has prompted debate on whether Judea and Samaria (also called the West Bank) with its large Arab population and high birthrate should ever be incorporated in the "Greater Israel." Some Israelis contend that should Jews lose their majority status they could no longer claim to be called a Jewish State. Others claim that a Jewish State does not depend primarily on numerical superiority but is based on historical considerations and on the quality of Jewish life that must continue to be maintained by the Jewish population.

AFTERWORD

After reviewing some of the many myths and misconceptions that continue to circulate in the community, I conclude with a few affirmative characteristics which I believe have contributed to the unique strength and continued vitality of Judaism.

We have been given a glimpse of the consistent openness with which ideas were discussed by Jewish sages. They were not reluctant to express their candid views on the most sensitive topics. For example, their treatment of delicate matters of sex was not a source of embarrassment, nor did they hesitate to come to grips with the problem of God's management of the universe. Almost no subject was off limits.

Moreover, they would ask disturbing questions and, by inference, would encourage their disciples to follow their example, provided the disciples' intentions to learn were genuine. Even when answers eluded them, they were not deterred from continuing their quest. Posing the right question would often prove to be just as rewarding as finding an answer. We are reminded of the curious child who approached his father with a barrage of questions which the father could not answer. Yet the father encouraged the child to continue asking. He reminded the child, "How else are you going to learn, my son!"

Related to the spirit of candor and inquisitiveness among our ancestors was their acceptance of a wide range of personal religious beliefs. Indeed, there were brief periods in Jewish history when Jews were ostracized by community leaders for expressing heretical ideas. Elisha ben Abuya in the period of the Mishna and Baruch Spinoza in seventeenth-century Holland were both excluded from community life for disseminating what were considered heresies, but such extreme measures were notable exceptions.

As a rule, a Jew's personal beliefs, no matter how extreme, were tolerated by the community leaders. The rabbinic authorities were more concerned with maintaining community discipline in the area of observance. They refrained from taking any kind of formal action against a member of the community unless he flaunted his rebelliousness by publicly violating the Sabbath or holy days.

Abraham Isaac Kook (1865-1935), the Ashkenazi chief rabbi of Palestine, asked why the *tefillah* (phylactery) placed on the forehead contains four sections of parchment whereas the phylactery placed on the arm contains only one section. He offered the following interpretation: In matters of religious thought a variety of views are acceptable; when action is called for, however, the community must respond as one.

We have also noted that throughout their long history Jews have thrived on argumentation, seeing no need to apologize for controversy. However, they distinguished between purposeful controversies and those that were self-serving and tended to destroy relationships.

Arguments based on ideology and reflecting sincere differences of opinion motivated the students to search more diligently in the sacred texts to find support for their opinions; they challenged their colleagues with whom they differed to do the same.

Outside the academies as well, community leaders and their followers were known to debate ideological issues with passion. No one was immune from challenge or criticism. Even the closest friends would take issue with on another without necessarily losing their mutual respect for each other.

We cannot picture what the Jewish community will look like in the remote future—enormous changes are taking place with such rapidity—but we can safely predict that controversies will not abate wherever Jews live. We can only hope that debates will be centered on ideological differences rather than petty issues.

Of all the values identified with Jewish tradition the infinite worth of the individual is most basic. The spark of divinity within each person confers upon him uniqueness and indispensability.

Jews do not customarily count individuals who comprise a *minyan* (quorum of ten for a religious service). Instead we resort to an indirect method of "counting the house." We say, "not one, not two," etc. Abraham Heschel, a leading theologian and social activist, explained to his students his understanding of this unusual custom: Because of the infinite value of each person, we are not permitted to reduce him to a finite number.

Saving a single life from destruction is tantamount to saving the universe, since each of us is a microcosm of the world. The observance of any religious law may be temporarily set aside to preserve a single life. Although we are cautioned not to assume that we can determine the relative value of the different commandments since we cannot know God's priorities, few would argue that to preserve a life assumes the highest priority on the scale of Jewish values. And to help preserve or restore another's human dignity is closely associated with the preservation of life itself. A life deprived of dignity loses its uniquely human quality.

Jewish thought cannot be confined to a neat philosophic system or theme. Our forbears were not primarily philosophers. With few exceptions they did not concern themselves with systematizing Jewish ideas. And yet, throughout the vast complexity of teachings one unyielding concept pervades every text: The sanctity and dignity of the individual. The rest is commentary.